THE NEW CONSTITUTION OF INDIA

COURTENAY ILBERT

GYAN

Published by

Gyan Publishing House
5, Ansari Road
Daryaganj, New Delhi-110002
Phone: 011-47034999, 9811692060
E-mail: books@gyanbooks.com

Distribution Network
gyanbooks.com
India, USA, Canada, UK, Australia

ISBN: 978-93-7097-310-7 (PB)
First Published, 1923

2nd Impression 2025

Printed at: Gyan Press, Delhi.

THE NEW CONSTITUTION OF INDIA
ARTHUR COURTENAY ILBERT

THE NEW CONSTITUTION OF INDIA

THE NEW CONSTITUTION OF INDIA

THE NEW CONSTITUTION OF INDIA

BEING THREE RHODES LECTURES

BY

SIR COURTENAY ILBERT

AND THREE BY

RT. HON. LORD MESTON

DELIVERED AT UNIVERSITY OF LONDON, UNIVERSITY COLLEGE, SESSION 1921–1922

LONDON
UNIVERSITY OF LONDON PRESS, LTD.
17 WARWICK SQUARE, E.C.4
1923

CONTENTS

THREE LECTURES BY SIR COURTENAY ILBERT

THREE LECTURES BY THE RT. HON. LORD MESTON

APPENDICES

NOTE TO LECTURES I, II, AND III

The three lectures for which I am responsible are not what I had hoped and intended to make them. Unexpected, severe and prolonged illness placed difficulties almost insuperable in the way of their preparation, made personal delivery of them impossible, and prevented me from revising them. For their delivery on my behalf I owe a debt of gratitude to my daughter, Mrs. Herbert Fisher.

C. P. ILBERT.

LECTURES BY

SIR COURTENAY ILBERT

FORMING

LECTURE I: Preliminary

LECTURE II: The Provincial Governments

LECTURE III: The Central Governments

THE

NEW CONSTITUTION OF INDIA

LECTURE I

PRELIMINARY

WHEN Sir Gregory Foster asked me last Christmas, on behalf of the authorities of University College, to give two or three lectures on the new Indian Constitution under the Act of 1919, I appreciated the compliment highly. But I felt many doubts and misgivings about my ability to perform the task. The subject is big, difficult, controversial—very big, very difficult, very controversial. What justification can an octogenarian plead, what excuse can he offer, for attempting such a task? One justification I cannot plead. I have no right to speak to you about the India of to-day, because it is an India of which

I have no first-hand knowledge, which I know only from hearsay. Therefore I cannot give you any of those descriptions of present-day India, its phases and conditions, social, economic and political, which have made Sir Valentine Chirol's last book such delightful reading. I left India towards the end of 1886, and have never had the good fortune of revisiting it. And all my friends who know India best assure me that between the India of the eighties and the India of to-day there is such a gulf that impressions drawn from experiences of the India of the eighties would be utterly misleading if applied to the India of to-day. The only excuse I can offer for myself is that at various times during the last forty years or so I have been compelled to devote some attention to the history of parliamentary legislation for India. So it is from that point of view, the general constitutional rather than the special Indian point of view, the point of view of Westminster rather than that of Delhi, that I must approach my subject. All that I can do within the limited time at my disposal is to touch very lightly on a few of its many aspects.

I propose in the first lecture to speak about the factors which brought about a change in the British policy of governing India, and then, in the two following lectures, to say something about the new system of Indian provincial government, and the new system of Indian central government.

What should be treated as the starting-point of the new departure made in 1919? For many purposes it is convenient to take as that starting-point Mr. Montagu's announcement, or pronouncement, or declaration, of August 20, 1917. He then struck the keynote of the policy embodied rather more than two years later in an Act of Parliament. His was the first authoritative statement of that policy. When Mr. Montagu made it in the House of Commons he spoke as Secretary of State for India; and spoke on behalf of the British Cabinet, of the India Office, and of the Government of India. Therefore he spoke with the fullest ministerial authority and responsibility. His statement was afterwards fully reproduced in the preamble to the Act of 1919, and as that preamble carries with it, not merely ministerial but parliamentary authority, and constitutes the pledge given by Parliament to the people of India, his statement had better be quoted in the form in which it is so reproduced. The preamble runs as follows:

"Whereas it is the declared policy of Parliament to provide for the increasing association of Indians in every branch of Indian administration, and for the gradual development of self-governing institutions, with a view to the progressive realisation of responsible government in British India as an integral part of the Empire:

"And whereas progress in giving effect to this policy can only be achieved by successive stages, and it is expedient that substantial steps in this direction should now be taken:

"And whereas the time and manner of each advance can be determined only by Parliament, upon whom responsibility lies for the welfare and advancement of the Indian peoples:

"And whereas the action of Parliament in such matters must be guided by the co-operation received from those on whom new opportunities of service will be conferred, and by the extent to which it is found that confidence can be reposed in their sense of responsibility:

"And whereas concurrently with the gradual development of self-governing institutions in the Provinces of India it is expedient to give to those Provinces in provincial matters the largest measure of independence of the Government of India, which is compatible with the due discharge by the latter of its own responsibilities."

Probably the first thing which will strike you about this declaration is the deliberate avoidance of anything like rigidity or finality. It promises an advance in a particular direction. But the advance is to be cautious and gradual. The nature and times of the progressive stages of the advance are to be contingent on circumstances. The new arrangements are to be temporary, provisional, experimental. Growth is what is aimed at, growth, not a static condition. The mode and pace of growth cannot be foreseen with any precision. Any attempt to stereotype them would be fatal to the objects in view. The new Indian constitution is not so much a new building as a tent. It is like one of those caravanserais which would be run up rapidly for an Indian prince to meet a temporary need, and which could be easily removed or transformed when the need had passed. Some of you may remember a well-known stanza in FitzGerald's Omar Khayyám:

> " 'Tis but a tent where takes his one day's rest
> A Sultan to the realm of Death addrest.
> The Sultan rises, and the dark Ferrash
> Strikes, and prepares it for another Guest."

But the time for striking this tent of ours is still in the future. Our immediate business is to make the best use of it that we can. When you look at the Act which embodies this policy you will find that everything has been done to provide elasticity, and to facilitate alterations when alterations seem to be needed.

Who was the real author of the new Act and its policy? That was a question on which Mr. Montagu had much to say when he moved the second reading of his Bill. Athena is said to have sprung from the brain of Zeus full grown and fully armed. But that is not how new constitutions are born. The papers laid before Parliament and Mr. Montagu's second-reading speech showed that the pledges given in 1917 were the outcome of long and careful deliberations both in England and in India, and that these deliberations were based upon suggestions proceeding at different times from many different quarters. Among such suggestions, those which come from the ingenious and fertile brain of Mr. Lionel Curtis take an honourable place. Nothing could have been more laudable than the zeal and enthusiasm with which he approached and attacked the Indian problems of his day, nothing more useful than the knowledge which he brought to bear upon them. His suggestions have borne ample fruit. But to speak of him as the author of the new constitution is to misconceive the situation. The honour of the responsibility for devising and framing it must be much more widely distributed.

There has been no real breach of continuity in the policy of the India Office. But for events in Mesopotamia Mr. Austen Chamberlain might have been called upon to undertake the mission to India which was carried out by his successor in office.

The most significant phrase in the declaration of 1917, that which created the greatest alarm in some breasts, which roused the most sanguine expectations in others, is the phrase "responsible government." This phrase is almost as conveniently and dangerously comprehensive as the phrase "dominion government" in its application to Ireland. What does it mean? What are its connotations and implications? Its adoption was probably suggested by its use in the self-governing dominions of the British Empire, and its origin, variations, and developments there are fully described in Professor Berriedale Keith's admirable book on *Responsible Government in the Dominions*. You will find there that the expression was first applied to the Government of Canada in connection with Lord Durham's famous letter of 1839, and has since been extended to all the other self-governing dominions.

Let me ask again, what does the expression mean? Responsible government, responsible to whom? Not merely to official superiors, though that responsibility remains, but primarily and specially to elected representatives of the people governed. Now in the self-governing dominions both the expression and the system which it indicates, both the name and the thing, are at home. Canadians, Australians, and New Zealanders understand the system and how it is worked. They are familiar with its merits and with its defects. They do not claim that it is a perfect system. No system of government is. But they believe in it as the best form of government which they know, at all events to meet the conditions with which they have to deal. The system has been extended, wisely and properly extended, to South Africa, where the great mass of the population, its overwhelming majority, consists of indigenous Africans. But the introduction of responsible government in South Africa seems to have been only made possible by imposing on the indigenous population, in practice if not in theory, racial disabilities which could never have been contemplated in India, which would not have been within the region of political possibility there. This illustrates the danger of applying to any country political precedents drawn from another. In the British self-governing dominions responsible government, the thing as well as the name, is at home. In India it is an exotic. It cannot be expected to live and grow there unless and until it is acclimatised. How can it be acclimatised in India ? That was among the problems which confronted the framers of the new Indian constitution. One difficulty, an admitted and a fundamental difficulty, stared them in the face. Responsible government in British self-governing dominions means a removable government, a government which can be removed and replaced when it ceases to retain the confidence of the elected members of the legislature. But could the existence of any Indian government be made dependent on the vote of the legislature ? The method adopted by the framers of the Indian constitution for surmounting or circumventing the difficulty was very ingenious. We cannot, they said, make the executive of any provincial government dependent on the vote of the legislature, and we will not attempt to do so. We will not apply the new system to the central government, to the Government of India. But we will apply it to the governments of all the more important provinces, and the mode in which we will apply it is this. In each province the domain of government shall be partitioned into two fields. One of these fields shall continue to be administered by the Governor in Council, that is to say by the Governor acting with the advice and assistance of his nominated executive council. The other field shall be placed under the administration of the Governor acting with ministers appointed under the Act. And these ministers are to be appointed from among the elected members of the legislative council. Thus, not the whole government, but certain members of the government, will hold office subject to removal in pursuance of a hostile vote of expression of no confidence in the legislature. The subjects handed over to the administration of the Governor in Council are called in the Act reserved subjects. Those placed under the administration of the Governor with his ministers are called transferred subjects. In relation to transferred subjects, says the Act, the Governor shall be guided by the advice of the ministers unless he sees sufficient cause to dissent from their opinion, in which case he may require action to be taken otherwise than in accordance with that advice.

Will this ingenious compromise between responsible and irresponsible government work? An impossible scheme, said the critics, an unworkable scheme! There will inevitably be a conflict between the two halves of the government, and the result will be a deadlock. But that was not the opinion of the judicious and experienced men who sat on the joint committee of the two Houses of Parliament to which the Act went after it had been read a second time in the House of Commons. "The scheme," said the Joint Committee in their report, "has evoked apprehensions which are not unnatural in view of its novelty. But the Committee, after the most careful consideration of all suggested alternatives, are of opinion that it is the best way of giving effect to the spirit of the declared policy of His Majesty's Government." The Committee thought it desirable to state the theory on which the scheme was based, and they stated it in the following words:

"Ministers who enjoy the confidence of a majority in their legislative council will be given the fullest opportunity of managing that field of government which is entrusted to their care. In their work they will be assisted and guided by the Governor, who will accept their advice and promote their policy whenever possible. If he finds himself compelled to act against their advice, it will only be in circumstances roughly analogous to those in which he has to override his executive council—circumstances which will be indicated in the Instrument of Instructions furnished to him on his appointment by His Majesty. On the other hand, in and for that field of government in which Parliament continues to hold him responsible, the provincial Governor in Council will remain equipped with the sure and certain power of fulfilling that responsibility. The Committee will indicate in the course of this Report how they visualise the relations between the two parts of the provincial government, but they wish to place in the forefront of the Report their opinion that they see no reason why the relations should not be harmonious and mutually advantageous. They regard it as of the highest importance that the Governor should foster the habit of free consultation between both halves of his government, and indeed that he should insist upon it in all important matters of common interest. He will thus ensure that ministers will contribute their knowledge of the people's wishes and susceptibilities, and the members of his executive council their administrative experience, to the joint wisdom of the government.

But while the Committee anticipate much advantage from amicable and, as far as possible, spontaneous association for purposes of deliberation, they would not allow it to confuse the duties or obscure the separate responsibility which will rest on the two parts of the administration. Each side of the government will advise and assist the other; neither will control nor impede the other. The responsibility for administrative and legislative action in their own field will be fixed beyond possibility of doubt on ministers and on the majorities of the provincial legislatures which support them; and they will be given adequate power to fulfil their charge. Similarly within that field for which he remains accountable to Parliament, the responsibility for action must be fixed on the Governor in Council, and he must possess unfailing means for the discharge of his duties."[1]

In the later paragraph foreshadowed by the words which I have read, the Committee attempt to visualise the new scheme, and to give a picture of the way in which they think it could and should be worked.

"There will be many matters of administrative business, as in all countries, which can be disposed of departmentally; but there will remain a large category of business,

[1] Joint Committee Report, para. 5.

of the character which would naturally be the subject of Cabinet consultation. In regard to this category the Committee conceive that the habit should be carefully fostered of joint deliberation between the members of the executive council and the ministers, sitting under the chairmanship of the Governor. There cannot be too much mutual advice and consultation on such subjects; but the Committee attach the highest importance to the principle that, when once opinions have been freely exchanged and the last word has been said, there ought then to be no doubt whatever as to where the responsibility for the decision lies. Therefore, in the opinion of the Committee, after such consultation, and when it is clear that the decision lies within the jurisdiction of one or other half of the government, that decision, in respect of a reserved subject should be recorded separately by the executive council, and in respect of a transferred subject by the ministers, and all acts and proceedings of the government should state in definite terms on whom the responsibility for the decision rests. It will not always, however, be clear, otherwise than in a purely departmental and technical fashion, with whom the jurisdiction lies in the case of questions of common interest. In such cases it will be inevitable for the Governor to occupy the position of informal arbitrator between the two parts of his administration; and it will equally be his duty to see that a decision arrived at on one side of his government is followed by such consequential action on the other side as may be necessary to make the policy effective and homogeneous."[1]

That is how the matter stands at present. The Joint Committee in their Report have expressed a clear opinion that the scheme now embodied in the new Act is not only desirable but feasible. The advantage of the scheme over the alternatives proposed by high authorities in India is its elasticity. If and where the list of transferred subjects is considered to be too small it can be increased; if and where it is too large it can be reduced. Whether and how the scheme will work, time will show.

The truth, I suppose, is that there is no constitution, however carefully and ingeniously framed, which cannot be made unworkable by an impracticable and sufficiently obstinate minority; there is hardly any which cannot be made to work with a sufficient amount of goodwill. I should be the last person to speak disrespectfully of the constitution of the United States. It is rigid, and is not free from the defects natural to rigid constitutions. But it has sometimes

[1] Joint Committee Report, p. 6, note on clause 6 of Bill.

shown a surprising amount of ductility and flexibility. The new Indian constitution is not rigid. It is eminently flexible.

The method which I have attempted to describe has become widely known as dyarchy; and about the name a few words may be said. The name is sometimes used opprobriously, as indicating something which might have been discovered in Gulliver's island of Laputa; sometimes descriptively, as in Mr. Lionel Curtis's recent book. It is a neologism in political literature, but it is not a novelty in the English language. Bishop Thirlwall, when writing his history of Greece, applied it to the government of Sparta by two kings. But it is still so much of a neologism that there are differences of opinion about the proper way of spelling it. Bishop Thirlwall spelt the first syllable with an "i"; but its spelling with a "y," dyarchy, seems to be coming more into vogue now. However it is spelt, it simply means dual government, and it might have been applied without inaccuracy to the old system of governing India, partly by the Crown and partly by the East India Company.

To controversialists the term "dyarchy" has done yeoman's service as a "bogy." In time, people will probably realise that the scheme so devised is only one of the many devices which have been tried, in England and elsewhere, for keeping the executive government in touch with an elected legislature. None of these devices has proved quite satisfactory. All of them have been uncertain in their operation. It may well be that this particular device will operate in a fashion different from and simpler than that anticipated by the Joint Committee.

Whatever may be thought about the feasibility or expediency of this method of applying to India the principle of responsible government, there is no doubt that any attempt to apply that principle to India is a grave, and to many a startling, innovation. The authors of the Montagu-Chelmsford Report, who advocated the new departure, did not disguise or minimise its gravity, or the risks which it may involve. The announcement of 1917, they say at the beginning of the Report, pledges the British Government to the adoption of a new policy towards three hundred millions of people. "We need not," they go on to say, "dwell upon the colossal nature of the enterprise, or on the immense issues of welfare or misery which hang upon its success or failure."

It is not surprising that men of authority

and experience in India should have viewed with alarm the adoption of a policy so much in conflict with the honourable traditions in which they had been brought up. In British India, some of them said, the ruling class are Englishmen, trying as best they can to govern a distant country, inhabited by foreigners, with widely different habits, customs, traditions, and standards of life. The system of government which was established in British India before 1919 had earned the admiration of the whole civilised world. It had been modified from time to time, no doubt wisely modified. The people of India, the natives of the country, had been given an increasing share in the administration of their country, increasing opportunities for influencing and controlling the government. But in essentials the system had been one of absolute government, administered by an experienced, intelligent, and impartial bureaucracy. Now this system was to be changed, changed not in detail, but in principle. How could the new departure be justified? To what causes was the introduction of the new system due?

The answer usually given to these questions contains, not perhaps the whole truth, but a very substantial part of the truth. The answer is that the great war which began in

1914 had made the trial of a new and admittedly hazardous experiment in India not merely justifiable, but unavoidable. It was a European war, but its reverberations and repercussions had extended over the whole of the inhabited world. It was a European war, but it was a war in which Indians had played an honourable and invaluable part. It had brought thousands of Indians for thousands of miles from their tropical homes to shiver and die in northern trenches. The stories of their sufferings and exploits had become household words throughout the whole of India. The war had breathed a new spirit into Indians and had filled them with new aspirations which could not be ignored. The problem of Indian government had been fundamentally changed. The war had not merely forced the pace, it had changed the conditions of the problem.

People still talk glibly about the unchanging East and treat the expression as embodying a truism. Is it not rather what Coleridge would have called a falsism? Is the East unchanging? Has it ever been unchanging? The East was the birthplace of the greatest religions of the world. Did their birth and growth leave the East unchanged? Did the conquests of Alexander leave Asia unchanged? Did the hurricanes of war and destruction which are associated with such names as Jenghiz Khan leave Asia as it had been before them? Or, to take a modern instance, is the Japan of to-day the same as the Japan of fifty years ago? No, the East is always changing, and in India as elsewhere the problem of the statesman is to adapt old institutions to new conditions. What *is* true, and it is a truth of which the Indian administrator and the framers of constitutions for India can never afford to lose sight, is that the traditional elements of society are of greater permanence in India than in most parts of the modern world, and that consequently political and social innovations are less easy to carry out there, and are viewed with greater repugnance and alarm. But to acknowledge this is very far from saying that India does not change. India does change, often and rapidly. And in a rapidly changing world the most dangerous attitude to assume is often that of standing still.

I have spoken of the new constitution for India as an elastic constitution. It owes its elasticity mainly to an extensive use of what has sometimes been called delegated legislation, legislation not directly by Parliament, but by rules and orders made under an authority given by Parliament. Ever since Parliament has taken to legislating for India, this method has been extensively adopted in dealing with Indian subjects, far more extensively than most people would consider prudent or desirable or wise for home consumption. The reasons for adopting it are obvious, and among them are the impossibility of enabling or persuading Parliament to afford the time necessary for the consideration of Indian details, and the importance of enabling alterations to be made without the passage of an amending Act. Nowhere has the policy of giving and using delegated power been carried farther than in the Act of 1919. That Act contains forty-seven sections and several schedules, and, when printed in the form in which separate Acts of Parliament are usually printed, occupies less than fifty pages. The rules made under the Act are conveniently collected in a handy little octavo volume, published by the Stationery Office, and occupy nearly three hundred closely printed pages of that volume.

The subjects with which the rules deal are of great variety and importance. There is an electoral code, running to nearly a hundred and fifty pages, and containing rules for the election of the provincial legislative councils, and of the central Indian legislature, consisting of the Legislative Assembly and the Council of State. Then there are the rules of business for provincial legislative councils and the Indian legislature, the devolution rules showing the extent to which and the mode in which powers of the central legislature are devolved upon the provincial or local legislatures, rules about the borrowing powers of local or provincial governments, and about many other matters.

One feels much tempted to touch upon the contents of some of these rules, such as the provisions of the electoral rules for the representation of different interests and classes by means of what are called communal electorates. These provisions present features of great novelty and interest, but to refer to them now would be to anticipate a topic which probably ought to be reserved for a later stage.

Mr. Montagu, speaking as Secretary of State for India, told the House of Commons that when he was at the India Office in 1917 he found, both there and in India, a general agreement in principle on the necessity for decentralisation and devolution, in particular for relaxing the control of the India Office over the Government of India, and for relaxing the control of the Government of India over the local governments. In the Act of 1919, as in ordinary official phraseology, local governments and local legislatures mean the same thing as provincial governments and provincial legislatures. For our present purposes perhaps it would be more convenient to use the word "provincial" as indicating that in India the province is the most important local unit, both for administration and for legislation.

The agreement about decentralisation and devolution was general, but it was only an agreement on principle. The details had still to be worked out, and they were worked out later by committees, such as the so-called Functions and Franchise committees which sat in India under the chairmanship of Lord Southborough, and Lord Crewe's committee on the India Office which sat in England. It is upon the recommendations of those committees that the Act of 1919 is based. As to the order of proceeding, it was felt that the beginning ought to be made with the provincial governments and legislatures. This accounts for the first chapter of the new Act being devoted to Local Governments. And it was strongly felt in some quarters that more powers ought not to be devolved upon the provincial governments, more independence ought not to be given them, unless they were vitalised by increasing their representative and popular character. Unless this were done the devolution would be merely a substitution of one bureaucracy for another. Of this feeling Mr. Montagu was an emphatic exponent. He spoke in the House of Commons about government by dispatch—that is to say, by correspondence between India and the India Office, for in this context dispatch does not mean celerity, but its reverse; and he said: "The only possible substitute for government by dispatch is government by vote. The only possible way of really achieving devolution and making the unit, when you have chosen the unit, responsible for the management of its own affairs, is to make the government of that unit responsible to the representatives of the people. If you simply say, 'Let us have an irresponsible government in a province, and let the Government of India not interfere, and the Secretary of State not interfere, and Parliament not interfere,' you have a policy which is merely the enthronement of bureaucracy and the very negation of the progressive construction of responsible government."

In these preliminary remarks I have been

trying to trace very roughly the sequence of thoughts, opinions, and events which led up to the new departure foreshadowed in the announcement of 1917, and embodied in the Act of 1919. What was, for administrative purposes, the India of 1917 and 1919? An English Act of Parliament, the Interpretation Act of 1886, defines both India and British India. The object of the Act of 1886 was to express in more general and convenient terms the most important of the special definitions which had occurred in previous Acts of Parliament, and thus to make the language of future Acts more uniform. I was the draughtsman of the Act, and I consulted my old friend, the late Sir Alfred Lyall, about the Indian definitions. We agreed to define "British India" as meaning "all countries and places within Her Majesty's dominions which are for the time being governed by Her Majesty through any governor or other official subordinate to the Governor-General of India." And we agreed to define "India" as meaning "British India together with any territories of any ruler, prince, or chief under the sovereignty of Her Majesty exercised through the Governor-General of India or through any governor or other official subordinate to the Governor-

General of India." We wanted to find some word indicating a kind of authority not quite amounting to sovereignty, the kind of authority which Sir Henry Maine sometimes described as semi-sovereignty. And we could think of nothing better than "suzerainty," little dreaming, either of us, that the word was in a few years to become the watchword of an acrimonious controversy in South Africa.

It was at one time the fashion to speak of the Indian native states as our Indian protectorate. The relation between the British provinces of India and the rulers of the native states in India soon superseded, for purposes of international law, the old-fashioned model supplied by the protectorate of the Ionian islands, and the term "protectorate," in the Indian sense, was extended to Africa, with very remarkable results. It is the declaration of an English protectorate over Egypt that lies at the root of our present difficulties in that country. Many have been the repercussions, political and linguistic, between India and Africa.

It is, however, with British India, not with India in the wider sense, that the Act of 1919 is concerned, and I must reserve for later lectures what I have to say, first about provincial government and then about central government in India. In this first lecture my first object has been to touch on some of the factors which brought about the introduction of a new policy for the government of India.

It is sometimes asked what justification there is for treating India, whether in the narrower or in the wider sense, as a single country, or its inhabitants as a single people. The answer is that the inhabitants of India are a congeries of peoples, differing from each other in race, religion, and traditions, and in the stages of civilisation which they have reached, but brought into unity under British superintendence. Such sense of unity and nationality as exists is largely of British creation. But it is there, it is probably growing, and no statesman can afford to ignore it. In a recent lecture delivered within these walls, Sir William Meyer, the High Commissioner for India—and who could speak with greater authority, knowledge, or experience? —said that he looked forward to a future of India as a great self-governing unit within the British dominions. I have tried to state fairly and fully the objections which have been urged against the new policy of 1917 and 1919. But I must not be treated as admitting the force of these objections, and I desire to express respectfully my agreement with Sir William Meyer's optimistic view. So far as my imperfect knowledge of existing Indian conditions entitles me to express an opinion, that opinion is that the new policy was sound, and was not only bold, but wise, in the interests both of the people of India and of the British Empire as a whole. A continuance of the previous policy had become impossible, a new departure was inevitable. The object of the new departure, the end in view, was government with the consent and co-operation of the people governed. About this there is general, perhaps universal, agreement. But about the best means of achieving that object and of reaching that end there is room for legitimate difference of opinion. It may be that the form of responsible government adopted in the self-governing dominions of the Empire is not suitable to the conditions and requirements of India. It may be that those conditions and requirements demand a different form of government. This also time will show. The new constitution for India is at present in a provisional, transitional, experimental stage. Its introduction was a grave experiment, but it was a necessary experiment, and it ought to be watched in a spirit of patience, sympathy, and hope.

LECTURE II

THE PROVINCIAL GOVERNMENTS

THE subject on which I have to lecture to-day is the system of Provincial Government in India, and I am afraid that I shall have to inflict on you a rather dry and technical discourse. But I will ask you to remember two things: (1) Constitutional Law is a dry subject; and (2) the endeavour to avoid, to steer clear of, the more controversial aspects of a topic does not tend to make the topic more juicy.

British India, as described in the Montagu-Chelmsford Report of April 1918, was then made up of nine major provinces and six lesser charges. The nine major provinces were the three presidencies of Madras, Bombay, and Bengal, the four lieutenant-governorships of the United Provinces, the Punjab, Burma, and Bihar and Orissa (Bihar and Orissa being a single province), and the two chief commissionerships of the Central Provinces and Assam. The six minor charges were the

North-West Frontier Province, British Baluchistan, Coorg, Ajmer, the Andamans, and Delhi. The three presidencies come first, first in rank and in historical interest. They had grown out of the old trading settlements, and each of them was under a Governor in Council. The lieutenant-governorships of the United Provinces and the Punjab had been carved out of the overgrown Bengal Presidency. Lower Burma had been formed into a chief commissionership in 1862, and, after Upper Burma had been added to it in 1886, the province of Burma became a lieutenant-governorship in 1897. Bihar and Orissa as a single province was a later creation. A lieutenant-governor was not then aided by an executive council, but was soon to have one. A chief commissioner was theoretically a delegate of the Governor-General in Council for the administration of a territory taken under his immediate management in pursuance of powers given by an Act of 1894, but in practice there was little difference between the position of a chief commissioner of Assam or of the Central Provinces, and the position of a lieutenant-governor. The North-West Frontier Province and British Baluchistan were frontier provinces, held and administered mainly for military purposes. Delhi obtained recognition as a separate unit of local government when the seat of the central government was transferred to it from Calcutta. The Andamans were a penal settlement.

Above and controlling all the local governments were, in England, the Secretary of State and his Council, closely responsible to Parliament, and, in India, the Governor-General and his Council, commonly called the Government of India.

Now the scheme of the Act of 1919 was to place the more important of these provinces in the same kind of position as the three old presidencies, to place each of them under a Governor in Council, and to call them "governors' provinces." But the scheme left out of its scope the important province of Burma. The reason was that an influential school of thought held that Burma did not properly form part of British India, ought to be severed from it, and placed in a position similar to that occupied by the Straits Settlements and Ceylon. This view prevailed both when the 1919 Bill was introduced, and when it was under consideration by the joint committee of the two Houses of Parliament. But subsequently, by an executive order, for which the Act of 1919 gave statutory authority, Burma was placed in the same, or substantially the same, position as a governor's province under the Act of 1919. The results are somewhat puzzling to students of the new Indian constitution. They will find that Burma is left out of the Act of 1919; they will find reference to it in the statutory rules made under that Act, and, if they have time to peruse the pages of *Hansard*, they will find that proposals to amend the Act of 1919 by extending it to Burma were made, but subsequently dropped. Whether those whose views prevailed in 1919 had at their back any important body of opinion in Burma itself, and how far the adoption of those views would have been welcomed by an over-burdened Colonial Office, are questions about which I do not know enough to express any opinion.

The Act of 1919 has remodelled both the executive governments and the legislatures of the Indian provinces. In so doing it adopts, with modifications, the recommendations made by the Southborough Committees which sat in India. The opening section of the first part of the Act regulates the relation between the central government and the local or provincial governments. It indicates the principles on which powers, duties, and responsibilities are to be devolved from the central government to the provincial governments, and leaves the extent and conditions of the devolution to be settled by statutory rules. It distinguishes between central subjects and provincial subjects, and again between those provincial subjects which are to be treated as reserved subjects and those which are to be treated as transferred subjects. The first section of the Act runs as follows :

1.—(1) Provision may be made by rules under the Government of India Act, 1915, as amended by the Government of India (Amendment) Act, 1916 (which Act, as so amended, is in this Act referred to as "the principal Act")—

(*a*) for the classification of subjects, in relation to the functions of government, as central and provincial subjects, for the purpose of distinguishing the functions of local governments and local legislatures from the functions of the Governor-General in Council and the Indian legislature ;

(*b*) for the devolution of authority in respect of provincial subjects to local governments, and for the allocation of revenues or other moneys to those governments ;

(*c*) for the use under the authority of the Governor-General in Council of the agency of local governments in relation to central subjects, in so far as such agency may be found convenient, and for determining the financial conditions of such agency ; and (*d*) for the transfer from among the provincial subjects of subjects (in this Act referred to as "transferred subjects") to the administration of the governor acting with ministers appointed under this Act, and for the allocation of revenues or moneys for the purpose of such administration.

(2) Without prejudice to the generality of the foregoing powers, rules made for the above-mentioned purposes may—

(i) regulate the extent and conditions of such devolution, allocation, and transfer;

(ii) provide for fixing the contributions payable by local governments to the Governor-General in Council, and making such contributions a first charge on allocated revenues or moneys;

(iii) provide for constituting a finance department in any province, and regulating the functions of that department;

(iv) provide for regulating the exercise of the authority vested in the local government of a province over members of the public services therein;

(v) provide for the settlement of doubts arising as to whether any matter does or does not relate to a provincial subject or a transferred subject, and for the treatment of matters which affect both a transferred subject and a subject which is not transferred; and

(vi) make such consequential and supplemental provisions as appear necessary or expedient:

Provided that, without prejudice to any general power of revoking or altering rules under the principal Act, the rules shall not authorise the revocation or suspension of the transfer of any subject except with the sanction of the Secretary of State in Council.

*   *   *   *   *

(4) The expressions "central subjects" and "provincial subjects" as used in this Act mean subjects so classified under the rules.

Provincial subjects, other than transferred subjects, are in this Act referred to as "reserved subjects."

Let me note one or two points in connection with these provisions. The rules made in pursuance of the powers given by the section are collected under the head of "devolution rules" in the little volume published by the Stationery Office to which I referred in my last lecture. They are of the highest importance, and no one who wishes to understand the mode in which powers, duties, and responsibilities are distributed in the new constitution between the central authority in India and the provincial authorities can afford to dispense with a careful study of them. The rules and the schedules attached to them enumerate forty-seven subjects which are to be classified as central, and fifty-two subjects which are to be classified as provincial. The rules and schedules must be read together, and in connection with the provisions of the

Act under which they are made, and therefore are subject to numerous exceptions and qualifications. A fruitful field, you may be disposed to say, for profitable litigation, profitable to the lawyer and expensive to the tax-payer. But the lawyer must not be too sanguine in his expectation of profits from this field, for everything has been done in the Act and rules to withdraw from litigation the questions arising under them, and to provide for their settlement by administrative action. Consider the wide latitude of administrative action allowed by the important section which I read to you just now,[1] and one of the rules, headed " settlement of doubts," lays down that :

> " When any doubt arises as to whether a particular matter does or does not relate to a provincial subject, the Governor-General in Council shall decide whether the matter does or does not relate, and his decision shall be final."

The authority devolved by the new constitution on provincial governments in respect of subjects classified as provincial, and the allocation to those governments of specific sources of revenue, emancipate the local

[1] 9 & 10 Geo. V., c. 101 (3).

governments largely from the parental tutelage under which they had previously lived, and make it possible for them to exercise borrowing powers on their own account. Such borrowing powers are accordingly given by a later section. Where the provincial governments act merely as agents for the central government in respect of subjects classified as central, their independence is naturally less, and the authority delegated to them may be withdrawn or modified as circumstances seem to require.

The Act expressly recognises the system of dual government or dyarchy on which I touched in my last lecture. Where there is council government, as will be the case in all the more important provinces, the Governor in Council will deal with "reserved subjects," but "transferred subjects" are handed over to the governor acting with ministers appointed under the Act, i.e. appointed from among elected members of the legislative council. The position of these ministers and the relations between the two halves of the government are regulated by later sections of the Act (ss. 4, 6). The Act requires that the administrative control exercised by the central government over provincial subjects shall be less in the case of transferred subjects than in the case of reserved subjects.

The constitution of the executive councils for the more important provinces, governors' provinces as they are called in the Act, is much the same as that of the executive councils for the three presidencies before the passing of the Act. The maximum number of members of the executive council remains four, but only one of these, instead of two, need have had twelve years' previous service under the Crown in India. The joint committee of the two Houses of Parliament had proposed that the executive council should consist of two ordinary members, one a European qualified by long official experience, the other an Indian. But this proposal was not provided for in the Act because it was thought undesirable to require by statute any racial qualification or to impose by statute any racial disqualification. Subject to the maximum of four, the number of the council and the proportion between Europeans and Indians will be settled by practice. But it is, I understand, contemplated that in any event the executive councils of the provinces will continue to include at least one Indian member, and that, if a second European member is added, there will also be a second Indian member. The old statutory provision that if the Commander-in-Chief happens to reside in Calcutta, Madras, or Bombay he is to be an additional member of the executive council for the province had become obsolete and is dropped.

This is as much as need now be said about the composition of the provincial executive councils. In the composition and functions of the provincial legislatures the new constitution makes important and drastic changes. The legislative council for every province is to consist of the members of the executive council, and of members either elected or nominated. Of the members of each council not more than 20 per cent. are to be official members, and at least 70 per cent. are to be elected members. A schedule to the Act fixes the number of each council, and it will be seen that the number of each council is much greater than that of the old legislative councils even after they had been enlarged under Lord Morley's Act of 1909. For instance, under Lord Morley's Act the maximum number of the Bengal, Madras, Bombay, and the United Provinces legislative councils was 50. Compare this with the numbers shown in the schedule to the new Act (Sched. I, p. 33):

" Madras	118
Bombay	111
Bengal	125
United Provinces	118
Punjab	83
Bihar and Orissa	98
Central Provinces	70
Assam	53 "

And even these numbers may be increased by statutory rule, provided that the statutory proportion between official and elected members is maintained.

Not merely in fixing numbers, but in other important points large powers are left to be exercised by statutory rules. Subsection 4 of s. 7 says :

" (4) Subject as aforesaid, provision may be made by rules under the principal Act as to—

" (*a*) the term of office of nominated members of governors' legislative councils, and the manner of filling casual vacancies occurring by reason of absence of members from India, inability to attend to duty, death, acceptance of office, resignation duly accepted, or otherwise ; and

" (*b*) the conditions under which and the manner in which persons may be nominated as members of governors' legislative councils; and

"(*c*) the qualification of electors, the constitution of constituencies, and the method of election for governors' legislative councils, including the number of members to be elected by communal and other electorates, and any matters incidental or ancillary thereto; and

"(*d*) the qualifications for being and for being nominated or elected a member of any such council; and

"(*e*) the final decision of doubts or disputes as to the validity of any election; and

"(*f*) the manner in which the rules are to be carried into effect;

"Provided that rules as to any such matters as aforesaid may provide for delegating to the local government such powers as may be specified in the rules of making subsidiary regulations affecting the same matters."

The mode in which these large delegated powers have been exercised is shown by the little volume of rules under the 1919 Act, especially by those grouped as "electoral rules." Lord Morley's Act of 1909, and the regulations under it, had provided for the representation of special interests, partly by nomination, partly by election. Elected members were returned by constituencies such as local municipalities, district and local boards, universities, chambers of commerce, and trade associations, and also by groups of persons such as landholders or tea-planters. Mohammedans had also succeeded in obtaining separate representation. The legislation of 1919, the Act of that year as supplemented by statutory rules, carries a great deal farther the representation of special interests, and for that purpose relies more on election than on nomination. The extremely ingenious electoral rules under the new Act will have to encounter the objections so often urged against the methods and devices of proportional representation, that their machinery is liable to be captured and misused by unscrupulous and self-seeking political wirepullers. They must meet these objections as best they may, and it will be borne in mind that similar objections may be and have been urged against the adoption of similar methods in almost every part of the civilised world. The objections against communal electorates and other methods of securing protection for minorities are frankly recognised by the Montagu-Chelmsford Report as having to be considered and weighed by all who hold that government ought to be based on popular representation. Autocratic government, whether by an individual or a bureaucracy, can always claim the merit of simplicity. With the perils which it involves all the world is familiar.

Those who are interested in constitutional experiments could with great advantage study the code of electoral rules under the Act of 1919, and might be advised to begin their study by taking some part of British India with which they happen to be specially acquainted and seeing how the rules are applied there. For instance, a student might begin with the Bengal rules, and the schedules attached to them, and discover what is meant by general constituencies and by special constituencies, such as the landholders' constituency or the commerce and industry constituency. He will find that, while an elector who has the qualification of a voter in special constituencies may exercise the vote for as many constituencies of that class as he is qualified for, he can only vote in one "general constituency," and even in that constituency his vote must be given by him, not as a citizen, but in some special capacity, such as that of non-Mohammedan, Mohammedan, European, or Anglo-Indian. To the objections which may be urged against this method of voting, on the ground that it tends to obscure the common citizenship which ought to be the basis of a political franchise, and to continue and stereotype class distinctions and religious distinctions which ought to be removed or minimised, full justice has been done in the pages of the Montagu-Chelmsford Report. But it must be acknowledged that the problem before the Franchise Committee which sat in India, and on the recommendations of which the electoral rules were based, was of extraordinary difficulty, and every credit ought to be given to the industry and ingenuity of those by whom the rules were compiled. The task of devising an electoral franchise adaptable and suitable to the infinitely varying needs and conditions of a vast population like that of India might well baffle the most experienced, ingenious, and courageous of constitution makers.

The legislative councils of the provinces have grown from being modest expansions of the governor's executive council into being large assemblies of legislators. This growth has necessitated a change in their relation to the governor. He formerly presided in person at meetings of the legislative council. He is no longer a member of the legislative council, but he has the right of addressing the council and may for that purpose require the attendance of its members. He has been withdrawn into a convenient Olympian height from which he can watch and control, so far as seems advisable or possible, the proceedings of the legislature. The duty of presiding at meetings of the legislative council is now performed by a president, who is in the first instance appointed by the governor, but will in future be elected by the legislative council, subject to the governor's approval. Both the president and the deputy president draw salaries, fixed by the governor for the first president, and in other cases by the council itself.

The object of the new constitution is twofold:

1. To emancipate the local governments and legislatures from central control.

2. To advance, by successive stages, in the direction of conferring responsible government on the provinces.

The first of these two tasks is easier than the second, and you will see that considerable steps towards accomplishing it are made by the first part of the new Act.

Section 10 of the Act deals with the legislative powers of the new councils. It limits the number of cases in which previous sanction of the Governor-General is required for provincial Bills, and at the same time makes the statutory list of those cases complete, so as to avoid continuance of the previous practice under which Bills not included in the list had to be submitted for previous sanction under "executive order." Absence of previous sanction cannot be made a ground for attacking the validity of a Bill which has received the Governor-General's assent. Consequently, legislative power may be distributed between the central government and the provincial legislatures without risk of the validity of provincial Acts being challenged in the courts of law.

An important section of the Act (s. 11) deals with business and procedure in the legislative council of a province. It declares expressly that, subject to rules and standing orders affecting the council, there shall be freedom of speech in the council, and that no person shall be liable to any proceedings in any court by reason of his speech or vote in the council, or by reason of anything contained in any official report of the proceedings of the council.

The general scheme of the Act is to give

the legislative council large powers of control both over finance and over general legislation, but at the same time to arm the executive government with the power of obtaining such money and the passage of such laws as are necessary for the proper administration of the province. The annual appropriations of money are submitted to the votes of the council in the form of demands for grants. If the council refuses assent to a demand relating to what is called a reserved subject, and the governor certifies that the expenditure is essential to the discharge of his responsibility for the subject of the expenditure, the Governor in Council has power to meet the expenditure notwithstanding the refusal. If the demand relates to a transferred subject the assent of the council is required, but the governor can nevertheless in cases of emergency authorise expenditure which in his opinion is necessary for the safety or tranquillity of the province, or in carrying on the administration of any department. Thus the governor can provide funds for any unforeseen emergency, and also, in the last resort, prevent a transferred department from being temporarily closed down on account of refusal of supplies. In accordance with British parliamentary practice and the precedents followed in British self-governing dominions, a proposal for the appropriation of provincial revenues or for incurring any expenditure under a resolution cannot be made except on the recommendation of the governor. The special powers with which the executive government is armed extend not only to the expenditure of money, but also to the passage of Acts. If the council refuses or fails to pass a Bill relating to a "reserved subject," the governor may certify that the passage of the Bill is essential to the discharge of his responsibility, and thereupon the necessary Bill becomes an Act on signature by the governor. The Act so signed is expressed to be made by the governor, is sent to the Governor-General in Council, is reserved by him for the signification of His Majesty's pleasure, and when assent to it is given by the King in Council and notified to the Governor-General the Act becomes law and has the same force and effect as if it had been passed by the local legislature and had obtained the necessary assent. An Act made by a governor under this exceptional power must be laid before each House of the British Parliament in such a way that either House will have an opportunity of expressing an opinion upon it. Of course it is presumed that recourse will not be had to this exceptional method of legislation until all means of obtaining the requisite legislation in the ordinary way have been exhausted.

I have inflicted on you to-day a dry and technical discourse, and I fear that I may have exhausted your patience and power of attention. But the subject-matter is complicated and technical, and cannot be safely described in popular language. The new constitution for India is open to the criticism that some of its provisions, though extremely ingenious, are too complex to be easily workable. I have sometimes thought that a well-known dictum of Lord Bacon might with advantage be borne in mind by those who frame constitutions, political or commercial. Lord Bacon says in his *Novum Organum*, "Subtilitas naturæ subtilitatem sensus et intellectus multis partibus superat." However subtle and ingenious the craftsman who frames a constitutional or legal instrument may be, he is pretty sure to find that he has failed to provide for all possible contingencies. Therefore he is ordinarily well advised in employing, as far as possible, simple and general language. As far as possible, for of course there are many cases in which specific provision is indispensable.

New constitutions have a disconcerting habit of working in ways neither intended nor expected by their authors. Constitution making is a fascinating pursuit, but the framers of constitutions must be prepared for disappointments and disillusions. The ingenious constitution framed by the Abbé Sieyès was diverted, or perverted, by the genius of Napoleon to uses very remote from the Abbé's desires or intentions. The South American constitutions devised by Jeremy Bentham hardly survived their emergence from the study in which they were conceived.

He would be a bold man who would venture to predict the particular ways in which the new Indian constitution will work or fail to work. Fortunately it is exceptionally elastic, admits of easy amendment, and is admirably adapted for the trial of experiments. Therefore we have every ground for hope and confident expectation that the trial of this great experiment will not be impeded by technical difficulties.

LECTURE III

THE CENTRAL GOVERNMENT

UNDER the new constitution for India the main differences between the provincial governments and the central government are two:

1. The bicameral system, the system of having two chambers of the legislature, is applied to the central government. The central legislature consists of two chambers—the Council of State and the Legislative Assembly.

2. The system of dual government or dyarchy is not applied to the central government.

Before 1919 the central executive government of India consisted of the Governor-General and his executive council, the central legislature consisted of the Governor-General in his legislative council. The new Act alters the constitution of both these bodies and the relation of the executive government to the legislature.

The reforms under Lord Morley's Act of 1909, often described as the Morley-Minto reforms, undoubtedly fell short of the requirements of 1919, but it is worth while to recall what they did, as showing how far they advanced in the direction pursued by the legislation of ten years later.

What change did the Morley-Minto reforms make in the central government of India? They increased the maximum number of members of the legislative council who were not members of the Governor-General's executive council from sixteen to sixty. In remodelling the constitution of the legislative council they expressly recognised the principle of election which had been latent in the regulations under the earlier Act of 1892. The Act of 1909 required that members of the legislative council should include elected as well as nominated members. The elected members were chosen by special constituencies of the same kind as those which I described in my last lecture as choosing elected members of provincial councils. They made the central legislative council consist of a single chamber, with an official majority in a total membership of sixty-nine members, of whom twenty-seven were elected. They materially enlarged the functions of the central legislature. Under the Act of 1892 there had been power to discuss the annual financial statement and to ask questions, but no power to move resolutions nor to divide the council upon them. The resolutions, if carried, operated merely as recommendations to the executive government, recommendations on which the government might or might not act. They extended the right of putting questions by permitting supplementary questions, subject to disallowance by the President. That is as far as Lord Morley or Lord Minto went in 1909, and they expressly disclaimed any intention or desire to advance farther in the direction of parliamentary or responsible government. But, as often happens, events were stronger than reformers, and the goal which was emphatically disclaimed in 1909 was as emphatically and authoritatively announced in 1917.

We are now in a position to consider the changes made in the central government by the new constitution as embodied in Part II of the Act of 1919, and the rules made under it. The most important change in the central legislature is its division into two chambers —the Council of State and the Legislative Assembly. The constitution of this legislature was radically altered in the course of the passage of the 1919 measure through Parliament. Under the Bill of that year as introduced in the House of Commons, the Council of State was a device for passing measures which could not be got through the Legislative Assembly. But the joint committee on the Bill held strong views on the utility of second chambers, and, in accordance with their recommendations, the Council of State became, to use the language of their report, a "true second chamber." Thus India has added to the long list of second-chamber experiments. A Bill is not to be deemed to have been passed by the Indian legislature unless it has been agreed to by both chambers, either without amendment or with agreed amendments. Provision is made for a joint sitting of both chambers. As in the constitution of the provincial legislatures, the Governor-General is not a member of either chamber, but has the right of addressing it, and may for that purpose require the attendance of its members.

Each chamber has a president. The president of the Council of State is appointed by the Governor-General from among the members of the Council. The Governor-General can also appoint other persons to preside in such circumstances as he may desire. The president of the Legislative Assembly is, for the first four years, appointed by the Governor-General, and is to be afterwards a member of the assembly, elected by the assembly, and approved by the Governor-General. The assembly has also, from the beginning, a deputy president, elected by the assembly, and approved by the Governor-General. Both the president and the deputy president draw salaries. The salary of an appointed president is fixed by the Governor-General, that of an elected president or of the deputy president is fixed by an Act of the Indian legislature. Both the Council of State and the Legislative Assembly consist of members nominated or elected in accordance with statutory rules. The number of members of the Council of State is not to exceed sixty, and of these not more than twenty are to be official members.

The total number of members of the Legislative Assembly is to be a hundred and forty, one hundred elected and forty nominated. Of the forty nominated members twenty-six must be official members. There is a limited power to increase, by statutory rule, the number of members, and to vary the proportion between the classes to which they belong. The life of the Council of State continues for five years, that of the Legislative Assembly for three years. But the Governor-General may dissolve either chamber, or, in special circumstances, extend its life. After a dissolution the interval before the next session of the chamber is fixed by law.

The Governor-General appoints the times and places for holding the sessions of either chamber of the Indian legislature, and may prorogue their sessions. Every member of the Governor-General's executive council must be nominated a member either of the Council of State or of the Legislative Assembly. He cannot be a member of both chambers, but, if he is appointed to one of them, he is entitled to attend and address the other.

As in the provincial constitutions, much is left to statutory rules. Thus under s. 23 provision may be made by rules as to

"(*a*) the term of office of nominated members of the Council of State and the Legislative Assembly, and the manner of filling casual vacancies occurring by reason of absence of members from India, inability to attend to duty, death, acceptance of office, or resignation duly accepted, or otherwise ; and

"(*b*) the conditions under which and the

manner in which persons may be nominated as members of the Council of State or the Legislative Assembly; and

"(*c*) the qualification of electors, the constitution of constituencies, and the method of election for the Council of State and the Legislative Assembly (including the number of members to be elected by communal and other electorates) and any matters incidental or ancillary thereto; and

"(*d*) the qualifications for being or for being nominated or elected as members of the Council of State or the Legislative Assembly; and

"(*e*) the final decision of doubts or disputes as to the validity of an election; and

"(*f*) the manner in which the rules are to be carried into effect."

Again under the following section (s. 24):

"Provision may be made by rules under the principal Act for regulating the course of business and the preservation of order in the chambers of the Indian legislature, and as to the persons to preside at the meetings of the legislative assembly in the absence of the president and the deputy president; and the rules may provide for the number of members required to constitute a quorum, and for prohibiting or regulating the asking of questions on, and the discussion of, any subject specified in the rules."

The statutory rules may be supplemented by standing orders, and there is the same provision about the freedom of speech as in Part I of the Act, the part which deals with provincial legislatures.

The new constitution enlarges enormously the fiscal powers of the Indian legislature. It will be remembered that under the Morley-Minto constitution all that the central legislature could do (apart from its purely legislative functions) was to discuss the annual financial statement, to ask questions, and to make recommendations to the government. Now under section 25 of the 1919 Act the supplies are to be voted in the form of demands for grants. It is true that an important field of expenditure is tabooed for discussion. Let me read you the language of the section (s. 25):

"1. The estimated annual expenditure and revenue of the Governor-General in Council shall be laid in the form of a statement before both chambers of the Indian legislature in each year.

"2. No proposal for the appropriation of any revenue or moneys for any purpose shall be made except on the recommendation of the Governor-General.

"3. The proposals of the Governor-General in Council for the appropriation of revenue or moneys relating to the following heads of expenditure shall not be submitted to the vote of the legislative assembly, nor shall they be open to discussion by either chamber at the time when the annual statement is under consideration, unless the Governor-General otherwise directs—

" (*i*) interest and sinking fund charges on loans; and

" (*ii*) expenditure of which the amount is prescribed by or under any law; and

" (*iii*) salaries and pensions of persons appointed by or with the approval of His Majesty or by the Secretary of State in Council; and

" (*iv*) salaries of chief commissioners and judicial commissioners; and

" (*v*) expenditure classified by the order of the Governor-General in Council as—

" (*a*) ecclesiastical;

" (*b*) political;

" (*c*) defence.

" 4. If any question arises whether any proposed appropriation of revenue or moneys does or does not relate to the above heads, the decision of the Governor-General on the question shall be final.

" 5. The proposals of the Governor-General in Council for the appropriation of revenue or moneys relating to heads of expenditure not specified in the above heads shall be submitted to the vote of the legislative assembly in the form of demands for grants.

"6. The legislative assembly may assent or refuse its assent to any demand or may reduce the amount referred to in any demand by a reduction of the whole grant.

"7. The demands as voted by the legislative assembly shall be submitted to the Governor-General in Council, who shall, if he declares that he is satisfied that any demand which has been refused by the legislative assembly is essential to the discharge of his responsibilities, act as if it had been assented to, notwithstanding the withholding of such assent, or the reduction of the amount therein referred to by the legislative assembly.

"8. Notwithstanding anything in this section, the Governor-General shall have power, in cases of emergency, to authorise such expenditure as may, in his opinion, be necessary for the safety or tranquillity of British India or any part thereof."

The proceedings of the central legislature in India are now reported in a convenient octavo form, modelled on the official report of proceedings of the parliament at Westminster, and the pages of the Indian *Hansard* throw much light on the working of the new constitution. Specially instructive are the reports of the Indian budget debates in the present year. They were conducted under the restrictions imposed by the Act of 1919 and the rules and orders made under it. It was at one time thought that the action of the Governor-General might relax those restrictions, but the advice given by the English law officers of the Crown did not confirm that view, and it is now clear that the restrictions cannot be removed or relaxed except by amendment of the statute. The Governor-General exercised his statutory power by directing that special heads of expenditure should be open to discussion when the financial statement presented by the Government was under consideration. Accordingly a general discussion of the budget was held in each chamber and preceded the discussion of particular demands. In the Legislative Assembly the general preliminary discussion lasted two days, and, by the help of a time-limit on speeches, was brought to a conclusion within that time. The range of discussion at each stage of the budget debate was limited by statute, and the limitations thus imposed raised several knotty points of order and procedure which had to be determined by the president of each chamber.

Fortunately the two presidents found themselves equal to the arduous task of interpreting the new rules of procedure and determining how far parliamentary analogies were applicable and should be applied. The president of the Legislative Assembly had the advantage of being an experienced parliamentary hand, for he had been a member of the British House of Commons, and had made himself familiar with its practice and procedure. The criticisms of the legislature on government expenditure sometimes followed the lines of debates, or orations, in the Indian National Congress. But one was also sometimes reminded of House of Commons comments and criticisms, especially at times when a Chancellor of the Exchequer has had to present an unpopular budget. A deep substratum of human nature underlies the differences between East and West.

Another pair of sections (ss. 26 and 27) make provision for the still more difficult cases of failure to pass necessary legislation. These provisions follow the same lines as the provision made for similar cases when arising in the provincial legislatures; and, when default is made by the central legislature, the Governor-General can, like the provincial governor, make an Act which, if approved in

England, has the same effect as an Act passed by the Indian legislature.

The new Act deals not only with the central legislature, but also with the composition of the Governor-General's executive council. But the alterations made in the composition of that council are not so important as the provisions made for reconstituting the composition and procedure of the legislature. Under the law as it stood before 1919 the number of ordinary members of the Governor-General's executive council was limited to six, and was in fact six. That statutory limit is now removed. There were also extraordinary members, such as the Commander-in-Chief. The qualifications for the post of legal member of council, the post which I once held, are altered. Formerly the legal member had to be an English barrister or Scottish advocate of five years' standing. Now his standing must be ten years, and a pleader of the Indian High Court of ten years' standing is also qualified for the post. The provision that when a provincial executive council assembled in a province having a governor, the governor was to be an extraordinary member of that council was repealed by the Act of 1919 as obsolete. A similar provision for the Governor-General's executive council is by Part II of the Act also repealed. Therefore when the Governor-General's executive council sits at Simla the governor of the Punjab is no longer a member of the council.

The Governor-General may at his discretion appoint, from among the members of the Indian Legislative Assembly, council secretaries, whose business is to assist the members of his executive council, and who draw such salaries as may be provided by the Indian legislature. This provision follows a similar provision in the part of the Act which deals with provincial governors.

I have tried to summarise very briefly, and I fear too technically, the leading provisions to be found in the first two parts of the Act of 1919, under the heading of Local Government, that is to say the Indian Provincial Governments, and the Government of India, that is to say the Central Government of India in India. But I am compelled, perhaps by bad arrangement on my part, to leave untouched the very important provisions made by the later portions of the Act. For instance, I have said nothing about Part III of the Act, which deals with what, from the London point of view, may be called the Home Government of India. This part changes the relations of the Secretary to the

Parliament which sits at Westminster, remodels the constitution and procedure of the Council of India, relaxes the control of the India Office over authorities in India, and sets up a new office, the holder of which is charged with important functions, and styled the High Commissioner for India.

The transfer of certain Indian expenses from the revenue of India to money voted by Parliament increases the possible control of Parliament over Indian affairs. Indian questions can now be discussed on the Vote for the Secretary of State's salary, instead of being reserved for the belated and often unsatisfactory debate which used to take place on the motion for going into Committee on East Indian Revenues. But it is to be hoped that the augmented power of asking questions about, and discussing, the proceedings of governments and officials in India will be exercised in the future, as it has been in the past, with discretion and reserve. Indeed, having regard to the increased powers, duties, and responsibilities of the Indian Governments, it ought, on sound constitutional principles, to be exercised with even greater discretion and reserve. There are many other statutory provisions, knowledge of which is essential to an understanding of the new Indian Constitution, but I must reluctantly leave them to be dealt with on some future occasion, and perhaps by another hand.

Part IV of the Act of 1919 deals with the Civil Services in India. Its provisions are based on recommendations made by the Government of India, in their dispatch of March 5, 1919; by the Committee which sat in India and is commonly referred to as the Functions Committee; and by the Joint Select Committee of the two Houses of Parliament in the Report which was printed by order of the House of Commons on November 17, 1919. In order to give effect to the principles laid down in the Joint Report as to safeguarding the position of public servants, the Act reduces to statutory form the main rights and duties of the services in India, and contains provisions specifically saving existing rights, and supplying means of redress to officers whose position is prejudicially affected. I understand that under the rules made for classification of services, three main divisions have been recognised: All-India services, provincial, and subordinate; that members of All-India services will continue, as at present, to be appointed by the Secretary of State in

Council; and that the same authority will have power to regulate the conditions of their service and will alone have power to dismiss them. It is, I also understand, contemplated that pensions for provincial services will be secured by legislation to be passed in the Indian legislature, that power to make rules relating to the provincial and subordinate services will be delegated to local governments, and that eventually local legislation will regulate these services by Public Service Acts. The Act of 1919 provides for the establishment in India of a Public Services Commission, which is to discharge in regard to recruitment and control of the Public Services in India, such functions as may be assigned thereto by rules made by the Secretary of State in Council. This commission offers interesting analogies to the Civil Service Commission which has recently been set up in Canada. But I have not had an opportunity of studying the rules made under Part IV of the Act, and do not even know how far they have been made and published, and when they take effect. Therefore I speak on this subject with very great reserve.

I should, however, like to take this opportunity of saying a very few words, not about the Civil Services in India as a whole, nor about the Indian Civil Service in its narrower sense, but about the English members of the Indian Civil Service. It has been my fortune to have hovered on the borders of two great services, the English Civil Service and the Indian Civil Service, and there was sometimes speculative doubt on which side of the border I ought to be placed. I am old enough to remember the introduction of the competitive system for admission into the Indian Civil Service, and the plentiful crop of gloomy predictions and prognostications which it brought forth. Afterwards, when I was in India, among my colleagues and intimate friends were men who had been sent out to India by John Company, and men who had been sent out later as Competition Wallahs, and I carried away with me from India feelings of deep affection and admiration for members of each class. When I returned from India I succeeded Sir Henry Maine as examiner of candidates for the Indian Civil Service in the subjects of law and jurisprudence, and in that capacity made acquaintance with representatives of many generations of Indian civilians. I have watched with constant interest their subsequent career. Lord Meston, who presides over our meeting to-day, went out to India before, but not long before, my return from that country, and thus I missed the honour of counting him among the very eminent men whose acquaintance I first made across an examination table.

My Indian experiences lead me to take a more hopeful view of the position and prospects of English officials in India than prevails in some quarters. A period of transition from one system of government to another is always difficult, but the difficulties are such as my countrymen have usually had the capacity and courage to surmount. The old regime of "jo hookum" is doomed; the element of force, which is indispensable to the existence of all forms of government, must remain, but will, it is hoped, be kept, as prudent governments keep it, as much as possible in the background. There will be more scope for government by personal influence and persuasion. But have Englishmen, as a rule, shown themselves wanting in the qualities required for that form of government? Is it not more congenial to them, might not its exercise be more attractive to them, than the life of a bureaucrat? There are other questions which seem to need impartial and considered answers. We all regret and deplore the recent indications that there may be some falling off in the recruitment of English officials for India. But to what causes ought that falling off to be attributed? How far are the causes permanent, how far are they temporary? How far are they due to apprehensions about the effect of the new system of government on English officials in India, how far to economic causes which are operating far beyond India? Again, what real foundation is there for the statement freely made that Civil Servants in India have failed and are failing to receive from the Government the support to which every servant of the Crown is entitled for the proper performance of his duties? The answers to these questions are at present obscured by a murky atmosphere of acute and bitter controversies, and for that reason alone the questions demand as careful and impartial investigation as can be given to them. Facts are coloured by individual and class opinions, prepossessions, prejudices. This is only what human nature leads one to expect.

You will see that my attitude to many of these questions is critical and sceptical, as becomes a seeker after truth with only an imperfect knowledge of the facts. I am sceptical about the accuracy of predictions confidently made, sceptical about the ascription of causes to phenomena. But my scepticism is hopeful scepticism, hopeful because I retain a belief in the capacity of individuals and communities, Eastern and Western, to surmount difficulties which for the moment seem insuperable. A hopeful sceptic I am, and a hopeful sceptic I desire to remain.

LECTURES BY
RT. HON. LORD MESTON
FORMING

LECTURE IV: The Genesis and Principles of the Constitution

LECTURE V: Its Working

LECTURE VI: Its Outlook

LECTURE IV

THE GENESIS AND PRINCIPLES OF THE CONSTITUTION

A NEW Constitution interests the student of human nature no less than the student of human institutions. To the latter it appeals as a stage in social evolution ; to the former as a monument of man's aspirations or follies. It may possibly have been this consideration which induced the University College to announce a second set of lectures on the recently granted Constitution in India so soon after the same subject had been handled by the greatest living authority upon its jural aspect. Lecturing here in March, Sir Courtenay Ilbert[1] analysed the legislative basis of the new form of government, and explained how it gives effect to the intentions of Parliament and of those who advised Parliament in framing the Constitution. He described the machine which has now been erected and he

[1] The lectures were actually delivered by Mrs. H. A. L. Fisher, owing to the illness of her father.

told how it differs from the plant which it replaces. What I propose to attempt is to supplement Sir Courtenay's narrative by sketching how the old machinery of Indian administration evolved, why changes in it were necessary, why the new plant is of this particular pattern, how it is worked and by whom, what are the dangers inherent in it and the safeguards against them, and finally what is the raw human material on which it has to operate. In this endeavour it will be for you to forgive me if I wander farther from the purely legal bearings of the case than would ordinarily be permissible in lectures delivered under the ægis of the Faculty of Law. My apology would be that for a full understanding of constitutional forms the lawyer must often dip into political history and national idiosyncrasies; in other words, he studies human nature as well as human institutions.

Regarded as a prelude to the present situation, the political history of India, during what may be termed the British period, is divisible into four stages. Divisible, in the exact sense, it may not be, any more than you can measure off the stretches of a great river which flows slowly on, picking up tributaries here and throwing out backwaters there, yet ever broadening as it moves. But the four stages appear to me to correspond roughly with changes of public opinion in England about our responsibilities for India—a public opinion which unfortunately is not based on progressive knowledge of Indian conditions, but has had to adjust itself hastily at long intervals to developments it had not suspected.

The first stage runs from the time when the East India Company first assumed territorial sovereignty in 1765 until they were finally divested of their trading functions by the Charter Act of 1833. During those seventy years the area of the Company's jurisdiction rapidly extended, without any correlative widening of their duties to the races who came under their sway. Between business and philanthropy the clearest line was drawn, and the scope of the latter was strictly confined. Order was enforced, and measures were taken against the worst forms of misrule: but the native dynasties were maintained, indigenous codes and forms of law were respected, and the religious and social usages of the people were left scrupulously alone. Whatever momentum remained in the administrative system of the Moguls ran on and ran steadily down: while the

Company stood by in an attitude of negative benevolence.

With the second period came a clearer recognition of the duties of sovereignty. Shadows of coming change had been cast before by the growing light of the evangelical and humanitarian influences in the English public opinion of Wilberforce's and Bentham's days. Christian missionaries, who had obtained their formal passport into India by an Act of 1813, were already leavening life and thought. Education in the same year, 1813, had been for the first time endowed, even if only to an extent which now seems microscopic, by an annual grant of £10,000. The vernacular press had been born in 1818. The stage was set for what Macaulay, in one of his longest speeches in the House of Commons, thus described: "We have to engraft on despotism those blessings which are the natural fruits of liberty." And this is what the Company and Parliament between them now proceeded to do. Their first demonstration was the Charter Act of 1833, which organised the provinces, consolidated the legislative powers of the Indian Government, and introduced a period of administrative efficiency and progress. Simultaneously, the Governor-General of the day, Lord

William Cavendish-Bentinck, was vigorously assailing the former attitude of *laissez-faire* and carrying reform into many departments of India's life. Our ideals of law, education, public health, and administrative methods were pressed upon the people with increasing fervour and, through the period which I am discussing, with increasing disregard of whether the people liked the insistence or not. The impact of Western civilisation, with its accuracy and promptitude and thoroughness in sharp contrast to the traditional methods of the East, was not to be a process of slow natural penetration. For there must be no delay, we believed, if we were to be true to our charge—the "stupendous process," as Macaulay described it in the speech from which I have already quoted, "the reconstruction of a decomposed society." It must be superimposition, not penetration; and what India itself wished became less and less important. In that long campaign of efficiency, unselfishness and high ideals were our armour: and I know of no literature more attractive, in its own stilted solemn fashion, than the records in which the English administrators of those days—names long forgotten by the outer world—reasoned out, from first principles, the application of the canons of justice and economic truth to the confusing conditions of India. In building up a new India on foundations borrowed from Western civilisation, there was no attempt to carry the people with us, or to enlist them in the ranks of social reform. So few there were who showed any anxiety to share our task, so little education existed or public spirit, that we lost the habit of consulting, or even of looking for, leaders of Indian opinion. Two other causes operated in the same direction. One was the apparent absorption of the acutest Indian minds in religious, rather than political, reform, and in establishing sects which aimed at purifying the Hindu faith. The other was the stunning blow of the Mutiny, and the disquiet subsequently caused by the Wahabi movement. Neither on Hindus nor on Mohammedans, did it seem, could we rely for disinterested co-operation in the task we had undertaken; and our only course was to carry on without them, and to argue out our policy over their heads. The attitude of mind thus formed was to remain with us long after the justification for it had passed away.

For the third stage, Lord Ripon's viceroyalty (1880–4) is a convenient starting-point. Tentatively, it is true, and with much dilution of its formulæ, the reactions of Gladstonian liberalism had touched a chord in India; and free institutions began to shape themselves in men's minds. Sentiment was fired by the dispatch of Indian troops to fight for us in Egypt, and by the warm reception given by the Viceroy to aspirations which, before his coming, had hardly been voiced. Two consequences directly ensued. On the one hand, an organised school of political reformers came out into the open: the National Congress was founded in 1885. On the other hand, representatives of the people were called in to the Councils of the Government. The former movement progressed with vastly greater rapidity than the latter. Each succeeding year brought louder insistence on India's right to share in her own administration, and generated fresh supporting grievances against the methods of autocracy. The appointment of an extra Indian member here and there to the small official legislative bodies was but a halting response, especially as the elective principle was steadfastly refused. This period thus advanced to its culmination under Lord Curzon, along three parallel lines—steady improvement in the machinery of the official government, a slow and reluctant admission of Indian influence in its working, and a growing feeling among the educated classes that the blessings of liberty were not being—and could not be—effectively grafted upon the tree of despotism.

The fourth stage of the developments which have led up to the present situation was ushered in by an outbreak of spasmodic revolutionary crime. Ascribed sometimes to Japan's victory over Russia, sometimes to certain of Lord Curzon's administrative reforms, the emotional outburst of physical violence which marked the early years of Lord Minto's viceroyalty had roots far deeper than any connection with those events. To discuss them would be beside my present purpose. All that is relevant for the moment is the effect which the movement had in awakening this country to the existence of a Nationalist spirit. The new Secretary of State, that eminent political philosopher, Lord Morley, was ready to recognise it. The new Viceroy, though neither a politician nor a philosopher, had plenty of quiet practical shrewdness. He knew when there was anything seriously wrong with either a horse or a man, and he was quite clear that something must be done to cure it. The obvious dangers of the discontent which was surging through India left the local authorities with no option but to advise at least an instalment of self-government. This was embodied in the Act of 1909, which instituted the form of legislature known as the Morley-Minto Councils. They were bodies very much larger than the old legislative councils, in which a handful of officials and two or three complaisant Indian gentlemen sat round a table and read manuscript speeches in turn. From those bodies they differed also in their powers and in their composition. They were allowed to ask questions with little restriction; they could discuss the Budget; they could move resolutions, raise questions of order, and divide the Chamber. In the central legislature, though greatly enlarged, an official majority was retained, in order to secure immunity against the risks of experiment in the body ultimately responsible for the legislation and finance of India. In the provincial governments, however, that safeguard was abandoned; and the benches were filled with a combination of officials, non-officials nominated by the Governor, and elected representatives of various interests. There was no majority of officials: but *per contra* there was no majority of elected members, and the provincial Governor could usually arrange his nominations so as to secure the requisite number of friendly votes. In spite of this and of the fact that the elected members were returned not by a direct vote but by intermediate electoral colleges such as municipal boards, chambers of commerce, associations of landowners, and universities, the new scheme was received with a chorus of approval and gratitude by Indian publicists.

For the disillusionment which followed, it would be churlish now to allocate blame. The Government of India have been accused of framing regulations under the Act which frustrated the generous intentions of the measure itself. This charge, however, ignores Lord Morley's own and very definite disclaimer of the parliamentary principle. He certainly cannot have meant the scheme to do more than it did. If he in turn is rebuked for thus compromising with the essentials of self-government, it must be remembered how difficult he would have found it to carry more radical changes against a suspicious and ill-informed public opinion here. So that the Morley-Minto reforms, with all their defects, went probably as far as was possible in a time of transition, and indeed served their purpose by bringing to a speedy issue the real constitutional problem.

What the Morley-Minto scheme did, at its

best, was to familiarise an increasing number of intelligent Indians with administrative questions. It provided them, through the right of interpellation, with facts which had previously been unavailable. It enabled them, by moving resolutions, to put the official world on its defence, and to elicit principles and motives for action which had previously been taken for granted. And it gave them, if they combined reasonableness with pertinacity in a discreet ratio, a considerable influence in the conduct of affairs. What the scheme did, at its worst, was to establish debating societies in which the official members had to vote one way to support their prestige and the elected members had to vote the other way for the sake of opposition. There was much unreality in the business. The budget was sacrosanct, and legislature could rarely, if ever, be passed in the teeth of the government. Resolutions on policy had no binding effect and the government could in no way be turned out. Hence much futile disputation, growing impatience, an endless faculty for irresponsible criticism, and a tendency to satirise the official executive for everything that went either right or wrong. With the lean results of constitutional progress were contrasted the successes of unconstitutional agitations in the west, e.g. by the suffragettes and in Ireland; and the arena which it had been hoped the new Councils would provide was deserted for the livelier forum of the National Congress and the Moslem League. The cry became insistent, first for Dominion self-government and then for home rule.

When the war broke out, the clamour was stilled for a time; but as the conflict dragged on, the fear grew that England would change into a great military nation with a leaning to martial methods, and the Indian politician decided to challenge us to extend to India the principles of liberty and self-determination which we were asserting for other countries against Germany. At the end of 1916 came an event of much significance. The National Congress and the Moslem League, hitherto kept apart by racial antipathies and divergent political ideals, met at Lucknow in the same week, within a mile of each other, and adopted a common platform of constitutional reform. Hardly less clamant than theirs, though never heard by the public, was another voice, that of the British official in India, pressing his Majesty's government for guidance in a situation of growing difficulty. Beating incessantly against him in his daily round, in the handling of his district or his province, was the real issue—what is the goal of our policy in India? Are we to hold it indefinitely and if necessary by force? Or are we deliberately to qualify Indians to hold it for themselves? During those anxious years of war it was of no avail for us to fence with those questions, to point to the general trend of all our past work and our professions; a specific answer was demanded by the Nationalists. The older-fashioned people, whose instinct was to support us, were being equally embarrassed; and in the absence of a lead from us, their active loyalty was being severely tried. The air seemed heavy with imminent trouble, unless an authoritative pronouncement could be obtained as to India's future. Such a promise was at last made in August 1917. You are familiar with its purport, the establishment by measurable stages of a system of government by the people themselves. With it my prelude ends. The policy of grafting on despotism the fruits of liberty had run its course.

From 1916, and even earlier, the ground is strewn with the debris of draft constitutions. Likewise with labels for abortive schemes—self-government, dominion status, home rule,

Swaraj. Out of the welter had emerged the imperative need for a new constitutional principle. The last announcement of policy by the British Parliament had been Lord Morley's: and the principle embodied therein, whatever it was, had broken down. The legislatures were not founded on the people's will. They could criticise and even influence the executive, but they could not control it; and to give them control now over an executive which was answerable only to the Secretary of State was impossible. A new and more logical principle was called for; and thus the keynote of the new regime was its assertion of the principle of responsibility. The word is not used in the ethical sense in which, for example, England is responsible for the welfare of India—that is to say, morally accountable to the tribunal of its own conscience. It is used in the technical sense in which an executive government is responsible to a legislature and the members of a legislature are individually responsible to the constituencies by which they are respectively elected. This import of the word is familiar to you all. If the executive dissatisfies the legislature, it is removed, usually by being refused the laws or the supplies it requires. If a legislator dissatisfies his constituents, he is not re-elected. Thus in the last resort an executive which displeases the people can be removed by the people. This principle, so axiomatic with us, is new to India. Yet it was Responsible Government which his Majesty's government promised in 1917: and the weighty discussions which proceeded from then continuously until the new constitution was enacted in December 1919 were mainly directed at considering how far, and by what method, responsible government, if it could not be conferred *per saltum*, was capable of introduction by stages; whether, in other words, autocracy and democracy could be made to walk hand in hand, until democracy should learn its paces and could be trusted to walk alone. It was a question of unexampled difficulty.

I have said that the democratic principle of responsibility was a novelty in India. For a similar statement three years ago I was taken to task by Mrs. Annie Besant, who enlarged on free states and free cities in the past, on Maine's eulogy of the village community, on municipal government as a gift from the East to the West, and on the elective methods of caste government. I should not weary you by examining these speculations, even if I were qualified to do so. Caste disputes, it is true, are referred in many cases to popular assemblies, though in a very haphazard fashion ; and the village community goes on, all the world over, under almost any form of state polity. There are also traces of isolated republican states in ancient India : but they seem to have disappeared before the Christian era. And certainly during the period of conscious history there is neither record of democratic institutions nor tradition of elective government. Hindu life was regulated by only two authorities, the Raja and the Brahman, Church and State being equally autocratic. Mohammedan life, thoroughly democratic though it is on its religious side, has long been habituated to military absolutism in public affairs. To bring the democratic principle in the everyday business of administration down to the masses, was now the problem. Here lay the inherent difficulty of translating into practice the policy of August 1917. Let us see how it was tackled (*a*) by the Indian protagonists of reform, (*b*) by the British officials, insistent on caution, and (*c*) in the historic report, signed by Mr. Montagu and Lord Chelmsford, on which Parliament ultimately acted.

First for the platform on which the political leaders of Hinduism and Islam united at

Christmas 1916. It is set out in a series of propositions, of which I summarise the most important. The Secretary of State to have his London Council abolished, and to stand to the Government of India in the same relation as the Secretary of State for the Colonies does to the self-governing Dominions. The Government of India to consist of the Viceroy, with an executive council, of whom half the members shall be Indians elected by the legislature for five years, and the other half shall be appointed by the Crown, but not Civil Servants. In the central legislature, four-fifths of the members to be elected; Bills to be subject to the veto of the Crown; resolutions to be subject to the veto of the Viceroy, but to be binding if passed again after a year's interval; military affairs and foreign politics to be at the discretion of the executive; but the Budget and all financial provisions to depend on the vote of the legislature. In each province the Governor to have an executive council, of whom half the members shall be Indians elected by the legislature for five years; neither the Governor nor his appointed councillors to be Civil servants. The provincial legislature to have four-fifths of its members elected "directly by the people on as broad a franchise as possible." The provisions for Bills, resolutions, and the Budget similar to those for the central legislature. Mohammedans to have separate electorates and a definite ratio, varying by provinces, of the elective seats in each provincial legislature. The provinces to be autonomous, but to make contributions to the central revenues.

To the framers of this draft the difficulties of responsibility, as you will have already perceived, were clearly insuperable. The whole important question of the franchise they dismissed, in the provinces with a vague phrase, in the central legislature with an ambiguity which I have not attempted to elucidate. So much for the responsibility of the legislatures to the people; regarding that of the executive to the legislature, the scheme is even more elusive. The legislature is given complete control of policy. It makes the laws, gives or withholds supplies, and even enforces its resolutions, being in this respect more potent than our British Parliament. As its agent for executing its policy, it has a government, partly of its own choice and partly independent, but wholly irremovable. The Governor and his council, when once the Indian members have been elected for their term of five years, will be responsible to nobody, if the stipulations about autonomy mean anything, or to the Parliament of Great Britain if they do not.

Had deadlock and confusion been the objective, they could not be more confidently ensured than by such an arrangement. The truth is that the Nationalists had never given much thought to the will of the masses and how it is to prevail, or to the actual conduct of administrative business. Their prime anxiety—and not unnaturally—had been to get control of policy and to secure a larger proportion of Indians in place and power. Possessing already a good system of administration, they assumed its continuance as an automatic instrument; and as for the *aura popularis*, they had no apprehension that it would ever embarrass the comparative handful of educated men who will monopolise political authority for the next generation or two. But the result was that a scheme such as the National Congress and the Moslem League adopted would have been neither democracy nor liberty. It lacked entirely that chain of constitutional responsibility which is of the essence of both.

Let us turn, in the second place, to the contributions made by the British officials, with their outside knowledge of the Indian character and their experience of practical administration. At the outset, during the long and secret confabulations which took place under Lord Hardinge, they devoted themselves to projects for removing racial grievances and ministering to the growing self-respect of Indian Nationalism. More liberty in municipal affairs, the enrolment of Indian volunteers, the abolition of indentured Indian labour in the Colonies, the right to carry arms, and so forth, were urged as necessary reforms. But when it came to political machinery, the absence of any declared policy by Parliament paralysed initiative. The best that was offered was some tinkering-up of the Morley-Minto scheme; and even as late as the earlier months of Lord Chelmsford's Viceroyalty, proposals were made to the then Secretary of State (Mr. Austen Chamberlain) which, though meant to be liberal and progressive, would only have exaggerated the defects of that exhausted experiment. When at last a decisive policy was announced in 1917, the future began to be explored on wholly different lines. From the public services in India enthusiasm could hardly be expected for the complete reconstruction of an edifice which they had spent generations in perfecting. But they are entitled in fairness to credit for more altruistic motives. Faced with responsible government as the policy of the future, and searching for means of bringing it safely to birth, the conscientious Indian official reasoned in this manner : The great mass of the people is illiterate, and vastly ignorant and credulous. It will be many a year before the ballot-box means anything to them ; and in the meantime the idea of a political structure broad-based upon the people's will is moonshine. Nor is there any certainty that, while they are politically helpless, the people's interests will be best served by the lawyers and landlords who will at first fill the seats of power. We cannot count therefore on the theory of responsibility functioning in the wider issues affecting the people's welfare or over the extended area of a large province. And what of the only classes who can be called in to a share in the government ? They have shown themselves acute and often industrious critics ; but criticism is not the qualification needed for driving the heavy and delicate engine of Indian administration. They will be handicapped by racial differences and social entanglements. In their inexperience, and even with the best will in the world, they will make terrible mistakes and undo much that the British rule has secured for the welfare of the people.

Arguing thus, the official advisers, with a few exceptions, played for caution. Their plea was for two essential preliminaries—the education of the electorate, and some training in practical administration for the political leaders. To many it seemed that an extension of the facilities for local self-government would provide the latter ; others were prepared to see parliamentary institutions established for certain departments of the administration and in areas smaller and more manageable than the existing provinces. Officials however had not the opportunities for conference and the concerting of schemes which are enjoyed by politicians ; and I cannot refer you to any single agreed project as embodying their views and their cautions. Such a project was indeed formulated by a meeting of the heads of the provinces while Mr. Montagu was in Delhi ; but I fancy that the seal of official secrecy still rests upon it.

You have now before you some estimate of the materials on which Mr. Montagu and Lord Chelmsford, with their respective staffs of advisers, set to work to prepare their report to Parliament. There was at their disposal an enormous volume of written and spoken opinions from all and sundry—gigantic tomes which will rest in peace till the white ant and the boreworm devour them, in the record-rooms at Delhi. But I have narrated enough to show you the genesis of the new Constitution. Our Government of India had steadily grown from the rôle of a cynical policeman to the position of an earthly providence. But the time came when the excellences of our rule could no longer be a complete justification for its wholly alien character. The very enforcement of our ideals had taught India to claim a share in the management of its own affairs. This claim we had met, tentatively and partially, to the extent of providing a small section of the English-speaking classes with occasions for studying and criticising our methods. But there had been no training in the combined duties of framing and executing policy; and when the time came for conceding India's political claims, this lack of training made it clear that we could only abdicate by degrees as the Indian leaders showed their fitness to replace us. Simultaneously the absence of an intelligent electorate precluded us from the grant of that complete political liberty which we profess to believe can be wisely used for democracy alone. This in a nutshell was the problem for which the Secretary of State and the Viceroy strove to find a solution in the winter of 1917–18. Their reply was contained in the report, dated April 22, 1918—a document of rare literary grace and human interest. The report was subsequently hammered out on the anvil of administrative feasibility by the Government of India and the provincial governments. It was then translated into a Bill and regulations; and these were subjected to a searching inquiry by a committee of both Houses of Parliament. Before the original *projet de loi* came on to the Statute Book, therefore, it was modified and altered in many ways: but the main principles survived, and it is only to them that I would invite your consideration, dismissing in a few words those changes in the old dispensation which, though of much import in themselves, involve no wide constitutional issue.

Among such lesser changes is the creation of a Governor and executive council in those provinces which were formerly under one-man rule. In each province half the members of the executive council are Indians appointed by the Crown in the same manner as their English colleagues; and incidentally I may here note that the same procedure applies to Indian gentlemen appointed to the Viceroy's executive council. A point of some importance is involved, to which I shall return later. Next among the minor reforms is to be the transfer of the whole machine of local self-government, municipal and rural boards, to popular control. This can be effected under the existing laws, or such modifications of them as the provincial legislatures are themselves competent to enact. And finally perhaps I may mention the steady replacement, up to a fixed ratio, of English recruitment by the selection of Indians for the public services. This is being secured automatically by the hesitation of many young Englishmen to adopt an Indian career while the political sky continues to be overclouded as it is at present.

The three major constitutional changes remain for discussion. They are:

(1) The Council of Princes;

(2) The bicameral legislature for the central government; and

(3) The dual government or dyarchy in the provinces.

For discussing the first of these, a convenient occasion will arise later. But you will see at once how impossible it would have been to leave the Indian States out of the purview of the new arrangements. They occupy roughly a third of India. The largest of them is half as big again as Greece, with a population half as big again as that of Turkey; the smallest of them is only a few acres of land: but between these extremes range a great variety of quasi-independent sovereignties, all deeply interested in the movements which stir British India. The conception of a chamber of ruling princes, by which they could be brought into touch with our policy and its problems, had long been mooted, and has now been realised. The chamber has of course no voice in the administration of our territories, and is confined ostensibly to matters of common interest to its own members and the areas over which they rule.

The second great change which results in the new central legislature was a compromise between two opposing arguments. On one side spoke the cautious mover, the brooder over foreign complications which may await a new Asiatic power, the British capitalist, and the industrial interests engaged in India. Experiment as you like, they said, in the provinces; but keep the central government with authority unimpaired for the preservation of order within and without, and with its powers of prompt action unweakened by dualism or any other untried device. On the other side argued the Nationalists. The policies which affect our well-being, they urged, and which accordingly we wish to influence, are hatched just as frequently by the central government as in the provinces. Railways mean as much to us as hospitals, and tariffs are as vital as industrial education. Therefore let us have a hand in directing the imperial as well as the provincial departments. Between those two views a *via media* was diligently sought. That some *via media* was necessary was impressed on the authors of the report by their belief that the position of the Secretary of State was to be materially modified, probably by the abolition of his council. This did not materialise ; but at one time it seemed near, and there was a feeling of awkwardness about altering the powers of the Secretary of State at one end and of the provincial governors at the other, and leaving the despotism of the Viceroy scatheless in the intermediate position. The course which was actually adopted discarded the idea of a dual executive, but attached to the Viceroy and his colleagues a legislature with a large elected majority and entrusted it with voting all heads of the Budget except those concerning defence and certain smaller charges.

In this way Indian opinion has its opportunity of influencing the policy of the central government. Controlling would indeed be the more correct expression, were it not that the Viceroy is armed with statutory powers to make a law which his legislature refuses to make, and to obtain funds which his legislature refuses to supply, if he is satisfied that such law or such funds are "essential to the discharge of his responsibilities," or, in an alternative and almost synonymous phrase, are "essential for the safety, tranquillity, or interests of British India or any part thereof." The second chamber, or Council of State, was intended to be a further safeguard. It is a small body, with a large infusion of official members, and such guarantees for sobriety in its elected members as a high franchise may be considered to offer in India. In a subsequent lecture I may attempt to examine how far these safeguards operate in the direction of maintaining the former authority of the central government.

It now remains to consider the new provincial system. It represents the supreme effort of Parliament, aided by many competent advisers, to reconcile the Nationalist claims with the difficulty of introducing democratic institutions into the least democratic country in the world. To speak in more precise terms, it provides the Indian leaders with an opportunity of learning the actual responsibilities of government by exercising them in a limited sphere: it furnishes the popular legislatures with a wide power to influence that realm of the administration for which the responsibility still rests with the old official government; and it ensures that the popular sphere shall be enlarged and the official realm correspondingly curtailed from time to time in accordance with the proved capacity of the popular leaders, and on the advice of periodical commissions of inquiry to be sent out by Parliament. The system has come to be known as "dyarchy," a term originally applied to it as a nickname, but so compact that it has remained as the accepted description, though "dualism" would be both more precise and less reminiscent of unfortunate historical associations.

In its mechanism and legal form, dyarchy was lucidly expounded by Sir Courtenay Ilbert in his lectures last term. He portrayed it from the point of view of a trained jurist watching it, as he said himself, from Westminster. May I try in this lecture and the next to hang below his picture a layman's sketch of how dyarchy appears to the administrator actually working it at Madras or Lucknow?

Its essential feature, as the name implies, is the division of the administrative work of the province into two fields. Let me, however, first make clear what is the scope of the provincial work. It excludes military matters; foreign affairs; tariffs and customs; railways, posts, and telegraphs; the income tax, currency, coinage, and the public debt; commerce and shipping; the civil and criminal law; and a number of smaller subjects of which the administration cannot be conveniently localised. All these are under the control of the central government at Delhi. Every other ordinary duty of a government is within the provincial ambit. It is this sphere which is divided into two fields, and these fields are placed under the administrative direction of two separate and mutually independent committees of government. In one field are the "reserved" departments: justice; police; land taxes and tenures; forests; the irrigation system; famine relief; industrial matters; finance; and several others of less importance. These portfolios are held by the members of the Governor's executive council, who remain as before answerable for the proper conduct of their business to the British Parliament through the Secretary of State. Whether Englishmen or Indians, these officials are appointed by the Crown, removable only by the Crown, and in no sense amenable to the directions or discipline of the provincial legislature. Their responsibility is ultimately to the British people. In the other field of the administration lie the "transferred" departments: municipal and rural self-government; public health, including hospitals and asylums; public works other than railways and canals; agriculture; excise; and various smaller matters. These portfolios are in the hands of Indian Ministers, who are chosen by the Governor from among the elected members of the legislature. They are answerable for the manner in which they discharge their duties, to the legislature; for if it shows that they have lost its confidence, it may be proper for the Governor to dismiss them and to appoint others in their place. Their responsibility thus lies ultimately to the people of the province.

Such are what, in familiar parlance, I have called the two committees of government; and such are the sources from which they derive their authority. In a sense the Governor is an *ex officio* member of each committee. In the executive council he presides, takes part in all their deliberations, possesses a casting vote, and is also endowed with a special power in rare emergencies of overruling his colleagues. He thus shares to the full their responsibility to the British Parliament for the proper administration of the reserved departments. With Ministers his position is different. By law he governs, "acting with Ministers," in the transferred departments. He acts on their advice, save when he has good reason for rejecting it; and they hold office during his pleasure. That is the constitutional theory, closely analogous, as you will perceive, to the observance of the self-governing Dominions. In practice his duty is to guide and counsel and help them, to habituate them to responsibility, and thus to let them have their way unless he believes them to be grievously wrong. He does not share their responsibility in transferred subjects; for technically what they are responsible for is the giving to him of advice which the legislature approves. In practice again their duties go farther than this, until they are indistinguishable from the duty of administering their departments subject to the moderating influence and experience of the Governor.

The dual functions thus outlined do not by

any means exhaust the obligations of the Governor. When an administrative question arises, as it constantly does, which concerns departments in different portfolios, it is for him to bring the two authorities together, to substitute consultation for conflict; and, where the matter in issue seems *prima facie* as germane to the one department as to the other, it is for him to decide in which department the decision shall be taken. Furthermore, when matters arise which are of such wide importance as to affect the work both of his executive council and of his Ministers, it is expected of him to convoke a joint meeting of the two committees, and in it to have the business thrashed out from every point of view. With all this, he has to be careful that there is no confusion of jurisdiction. Let an issue be debated by the full government or by any combination thereof, its final decision must always rest either with the executive council or with the Ministers, and by the decision the authority who made it must stand or fall. For this reason, although every order of the provincial authority purports to be an order of the government, the Governor has to ensure that it bears the sign manual of that particular half of his government which passed it.

Vis-à-vis the legislature, the two committees are in the same position. Each must defend its own policy, promote its own laws, seek its own supply. But the executive council, being responsible not to the legislature but to the Secretary of State, have in reserve the Governor's power of overruling the legislature if it is obdurately hostile. Ministers, on the other hand, being responsible to the legislature, must secure its assent to their policy without having any bludgeon up their sleeves ; and if they fail, it becomes a question with the Governor whether he ought to dismiss them or, in the alternative, dissolve the legislature in the endeavour to get the chain of responsibility revolving freely again.

These very briefly are the outstanding features of the dual or dyarchic system. Speaking recently in this College, Lord Chelmsford, one of its two sponsors, explained that he and Mr. Montagu had fought against dyarchy as long as they could, and had adopted it only by the elimination of all other possible alternatives. I do not know that any apology is needed for being guided by a process of elimination in finding the solution of a perfectly new problem. But dyarchy has positive merits of its own, and not merely negative or residuary virtues.

Precedents for it may be hard to find; but are there many precedents for one nation handing over the civil administration of a great country to another nation, and being guided in the pace of the transfer by the transferee's success in its new task? Dyarchy has been devised to meet those wholly novel conditions; and the fact that it was not rashly or hastily adopted is all to the good. It must now have time to prove its value as a constitutional system. *Prima facie* it provides what was wanted—a training in the school of practical experience for those who claim administrative power, a means of gauging their capacity in the use of such power as they obtain and the maximum of protection to the people while their future rulers are serving their apprenticeship. The most serious theoretical argument against dyarchy is that administration is a seamless garment and cannot be divided. To this I will advert in my next lecture, when endeavouring to describe the practical application of the new system to Indian conditions.

One word in conclusion. Sir Courtenay Ilbert hesitated to say where the conception of dyarchy originated. The farthest back that I can trace it is to a group of students of the British Commonwealth, headed by Mr.

Lionel Curtis, who sat down with a few experts from the India Office in an Oxford Common-room, in the spring of 1916, to inquire "how self-government could be introduced and gradually and peaceably extended in India." The result of their symposium was a memorandum, drafted by Sir William Duke, in which the government of the province of Bengal is divided hypothetically into two parts and administered in close accord with the essential spirit of dyarchy as we know it to-day. It is a striking example of how by careful study and exact reasoning the germ of a far-reaching theory may be cultivated in our laboratories of constitutional science.

LECTURE V

ITS WORKING

In considering what I may call the *vie intime* of government in India, one sees at once two important respects in which it will be changed by the new constitution. The first is the position of the District Officer. That official, known as the District Magistrate or the Collector or the Deputy Commissioner in different parts of India, needs no introduction to you. He was the best product of the Indian Civil Service, the pivot of the whole administration, and, if he was a good man, the father of his district as well, and the guide and confidant of his people. Practically all the public business of the district passed through his hands. He prevented the different public departments from clashing or overlapping. He was the channel through which the needs of the people reached the government and the legislature. He was the agent by which the policy of those bodies was interpreted, and often tempered and adapted, to the people. No race of public servants in the Empire have done better or more humane work than the district officers in India.

But what they represented, though at its best, was paternal government. They were the necessary vehicle of a highly centralised administration. They stood for the strength and the benevolence of autocracy. With the new conditions this must change. So long as a field of the administration is reserved for the control of the official executive, the district officer will remain as now the local agent for its management. But, as regards the field transferred to the control of Ministers, his chief task will be to wean the people from appealing to him with their needs or protests in matters of policy, and to induce them to have recourse to their own representatives. In other words, he will have to teach them the value of the vote, and how to use it. It is difficult to conceive how, for a long time to come, the business of government is to be decently ordered without an official as the organising head of each district, or how law and order are to be preserved unless there is a chief magistrate in each district to enforce them. A capable man in such a position will still have much influence and power for good : but the old rôle of the district officer will disappear as the people become familiar with the new principle of government.

A second big change which the new constitution will bring is a great extension of statute law. India is honeycombed with codes and manuals of public business, which repose not on legislative authority, but on executive fiat. Suffering as we so frequently do in this country from administrative anomalies and discomforts which it is impossible to get Parliament to find time to rectify, we can appreciate the advantage of an administrative system in which the defects are capable of being amended as they are discovered, without waiting for the scanty leisure of an overworked legislature impatient of departmental woes. There is the further advantage of elasticity, in the field that is opened for test and trial, and unchecked experiment towards greater efficiency. Dangers too there are in the method : but they were largely obviated by the personal element. Officialdom was a small and intimate hierarchy, with traditions of loyalty and little finesse, to whom instructions were ordinarily as binding as laws. Yet with all these merits, the system was only possible under autocracy ; and to the Indian reformer it has long been suspect as a symbol of absolutism. " Executive high-handed-ness " is a constant slogan in the Nationalist press. As free institutions develop, prescriptions of law will multiply to replace it.

By way of illustration, let me refer briefly to the directions under which the land revenue or land tax is assessed. From the Moghul Empire we inherited the right to take from the peasantry for the State exchequer a share in the produce of all cultivable land, or a share of their rent-roll from such intermediary landlords as we found or, in certain provinces, created. In Moghul times this right was frequently exercised to the extent of leaving the cultivator only with sufficient margin for subsistence and the seed for his next harvest. By similar reasoning, a landlord would be allowed to retain only a commission on his rental collections. Such was the theory of land assessment to which we succeeded. It has been profoundly modified. The margin of profit left to the landlord, the ratio of his produce left to the cultivator, have been steadily increased; for we believe that capital returning to the land will fructify it, and that agricultural efficiency rises with the agriculturist's standard of comfort. But there is nothing *in law* to prevent us going back, at the next settlement of the land revenue, and taking 80 per cent. of the produce or 90 per cent. of the rents. Our whole system of assessment and rates of claim depend upon executive orders, and the jurisdiction of the ordinary courts is definitely barred out. The advance in economic wisdom which has characterised the land policy has not been the result of legislative decision, but of official enlightenment. To the ardent nationalist therefore its merits do not redeem the reproach of its origin: and the cry is loud for an Act which will embody the principles of assessment, and will be open to interpretation by the courts. The pitch of the land revenue will thus be subject to legislative revision, and its periodical fixation will become a legal process.

By these two instances I have attempted to exemplify the changes which will come over the spirit of administration under the new regime. It is now time to describe the actual working of the machinery.

The electorate need not detain us long. Out of the total male population[1] of British India about 11 per cent. are literate, and out of the total female population about 1 per cent. The ratio of literate males to the total population is thus under 6 per cent. With a very limited female franchise, and literacy

[1] I am working on the Census of 1911.

very often confined to the painful writing of one's own name, this figure of 6 per cent. would, according to the ordinary canons, be the outside limit to the number of intelligent voters. In effect the number of voters admitted to the provincial franchise is approximately 5⅓ millions or 2⅓ per cent. of the population of the eight provinces. Even this is the expression of a very low qualification. In one province, which we may take as typical, every person whose income is £13 6*s*. 8*d*., or whose house rent is £2 8*s*., or who cultivates land at a rental of £3 6*s*. 8*d*., or who owns land which pays revenue of half that amount, is eligible as a voter; and so is every retired officer, N.C.O., or soldier of the regular forces. It is thus clear, the conditions of Indian life being what they are, that we are yet a long way from democracy on the one hand, or any recognisable level of political intelligence on the other.

In the circumstances it is natural enough that the character of the electorate should have little relation to the class from which are drawn the candidates who seek their suffrages. For practical purposes that class does not go beyond the small section (0·6 per cent. of the population) who are literate in English. It is only they who can usefully follow the proceedings of the councils, and it is only they who have seriously taken to Western political methods. Rural constituencies provide landed magnates with easy opportunities for election ; but the conflict between rural and urban interests, which some observers believe will create the party system of the future, has not yet become acute, and the majority of the elected legislators are townsmen of the professional classes.

Coming to the provincial legislature, I can best describe it by taking one exemplar province. It has a council of 121 members. Of these 60 are elected by Hindus, 29 by Moslems, 1 by Europeans, 6 by land holders, 3 by Chambers of Commerce, and 1 by a University, or 100 members in all. The other 21 members consist of the two executive councillors, and 19 persons nominated by the Governor, of whom 16 may be officials, one a representative of the domiciled Anglo-Indian community, one of the Indian Christians, and one of what is known as the depressed classes, the humble, useful folk who are outside the pale of the Hindu caste system. In some provinces there are other "fancy" constituencies—nominated representatives of labour, of aboriginal races, and so on. The Speaker or President is at present an official with some experience of conducting public assemblies, who is busy in building up practice and tradition. In 1925 he will be replaced by a President elected by the legislature itself. The methods of procedure and debate in the council are fixed by statutory rules, and follow closely the essentials of our Parliamentary practice. Speeches are privileged, and the President has full power to preserve order. Hitherto the legislative output has been comparatively small. The old practice of putting voluminous questions continues, and the discussion of resolutions occupies much time, being a very natural way of hammering out new policy.

In the council which I have described no party system has yet been evolved: there has been a brush between the landlord interest and the lawyers, but no reliable indication of future grouping. The same is, I think, generally true in all provinces. What, however, is even more definite is the absence of any pro-government party, in this or any of the councils. If the Governor's executive has to ask, in relation to its own sphere of administration, for a law which is unpopular with the nationalists, it cannot count on anything but an almost negligible minority of votes in its support. Similarly, if it has to open a Budget which runs counter to nationalist policy, it cannot hope to obtain its funds. Were the Constitution silent on this difficulty, we should have the impossible position, so far as the "reserved" field of administration is concerned, of an executive government which is subject to two masters: to the Secretary of State, who can remove it if it does not carry out his policy, and to the local legislature, who can prevent it from functioning if it does not carry out their policy. What would happen to the hapless executive when the two policies are not compatible? To this conundrum the peculiar emergency powers of the government furnish the reply. They are both positive and negative. If the Governor, in his executive capacity, requires a measure which he certifies to be essential for the discharge of his responsibility (i.e. to the Secretary of State) for a reserved subject, and if the legislature refuses to pass it, the Governor can make the necessary Act: but, except in cases of great urgency, any Act so made is specially reserved for His Majesty's pleasure after being laid before both Houses of Parliament, and does not become law until His Majesty's assent is notified. That is what I have called the positive power. The negative power has various degrees. The Governor may veto an Act of his local legislature, or he may return it with recommendations for reconsideration, or he may reserve it for the consideration of the central government. Furthermore, he may prevent a Bill from being introduced, or an amendment from being moved, if he certifies that the Bill or amendment affects the safety or tranquillity of his province or of another province. So far in the matter of laws. With supply the procedure is simpler. Should the legislature reject a provision of money for a reserved subject which the government certifies to be essential to the discharge of his responsibility (i.e. to the Secretary of State) for the subject, then the Governor may indent on the Treasury for the necessary funds. Finally, the government may disallow a resolution, or a motion for adjournment, on the ground of detriment to the public interest. These extensive powers adequately protect in theory the executive control of the reserved field of administration. To what extent it may at any given time be expedient to exercise them in practice, is a question for the judicious Governor to determine on each occasion when it arises. In his Instrument of Instructions from the Crown which he receives on his appointment, broad canons of constitutional conduct are laid down for his guidance, and he is advised to avoid an *impasse* except when the safety of the realm or the essential well-being of the people renders it inevitable. But crises are not always referable to exact rule, and the Governor must be trusted to judge the circumstances and the temper of the hour. It is the historical tendency of the elective principle to encroach on privilege ; and there will be nothing unexpected in the legislature asserting a frequent claim to control, and not merely to influence, the policy of the reserved departments. Therefore, said the joint committee of Parliament which dealt with the Act of Constitution, let it be perfectly clear that the Governor's power " is real and that its exercise should not be regarded as unusual or arbitrary."

We come now to the working of the dual provincial government, or dyarchy. In my last lecture we left it between the horns of a dilemma. On the one hand, we were agreed that inexperienced men cannot learn the art of administration without being given, albeit in a limited sphere, the opportunity of actually practising it. On the other hand, we were decidedly disquieted by the argument that administration is a seamless garment which cannot be parted in twain without destroying it. How can one half of a provincial government be amenable only to the people of the province, as represented by the local legislature, while the other half is amenable only to the British Parliament, as represented by the Secretary of State? How can the ideals which the official executive will continue to pursue in the reserved departments harmonise with the new ideals which Ministers will endeavour to introduce in the transferred departments? And when they clash, must not the people be ground between them? Such are the awkward problems which the practical working of dyarchy has to solve.

In the solution we start with the all-important assumptions that the present agency in the districts for the daily conduct of public business will continue; that it will serve Ministers with the same honesty and loyalty as it serves the executive council; and that the Governor will insist that it receives the same consideration from one as from the other, and that it is not set the impossible task of giving effect to two conflicting policies. They are large assumptions to make, and throw a weighty burden upon the Governor. But, if they are fulfilled, they narrow down the business of harmonising the two halves of the government to the executive council and the Ministers themselves, and to the permanent officials who form their secretariat at headquarters. How an administrative problem which concerns both halves of the government would be approached may best be described by taking two concrete but hypothetical cases and following their evolution.

Let us suppose that the Minister in charge of Education has set his heart on a policy of compulsory primary schooling for all children up to a certain age. He will naturally talk it over with his permanent officials, and they will put the district inspectors to work on framing a scheme. The number of children affected, the number and locality of new schools required, the arrangements for training the necessary teachers, the curricula, and finally the probable cost, will all be worked out in detail, and summarised for the Minister. His next step will be to persuade the other Minister or Ministers to stand with him, so that they may present a united front in the legislature when the time comes. This arranged, the Governor will next be approached, though it may be presumed that, in a matter of this magnitude, he has been cognisant of the proposal from an early stage, and has assented at least to preliminary inquiries. Meanwhile the idea has got noised abroad, or perhaps the Minister has been engaged in propaganda in support of it. And mutterings have started. The peasantry are beginning to take alarm, lest their children be forced to school at an age when they are actively employed on the family holding by the humbler cultivator. The Mohammedans happen to be in a suspicious mood, and are starting an agitation for exemption unless religious teaching is provided, or unless schools are closed on Friday as their day of prayer. An outcry is rising against any compulsion in the case of girls. The district magistrates, to whose ears these murmurs do not fail to come, have been warning the executive councillor who looks after law and order that trouble may eventuate; and the Governor has thus been separately approached from this side. At last a point comes at which he considers it advisable to bring his whole government together for a discussion of policy. They meet under his presidency, for consideration, not for decision, as there can be no decision for which the two halves of the government are jointly responsible. The Minister for Education propounds his scheme and argues its advantages to the national progress. His colleagues support him. The member of the executive council who holds the portfolio of Law and Order sets out the dangers, the hardship to the poorer cultivators, the racial susceptibilities involved, and the impropriety of using the police as attendance officers. Then the member in charge of Finance challenges the estimate of cost, urges the necessity for fees, and asks where the rest of the funds are to come from. Amendments of the scheme are volunteered to meet the objections, and an education rate is sketched out. You can imagine a prolonged and often a heated debate, or possibly series of debates. In the end the Governor has to decide whether the issue is primarily one of educational policy or one of public tranquillity; and according to his decision the further development of the proposals remains in the hands of Ministers or of the executive council as the case may be. Supposing that he is satisfied that the administrative and financial difficulties can be sufficiently met, and that he therefore places the policy with his Ministers, it will then be for him to thrash out with them the character of the legislation required to initiate the policy. He will no doubt advise them to modify the proposals for cases of special hardship, to compromise with the Mohammedan leaders, and in other respects to make the scheme as little burdensome as possible, compatible with its main purpose of educating a future electorate. When he approves of the Bill which they finally determine to promote, his executive council will give it all reasonable support in the legislature. They will assist in rebutting unfair attacks upon it, and the Finance member will defend the provision of the necessary funds and commit himself to budgeting for them. But the Ministers will be responsible for carrying the legislature with them, and for getting the Bill passed. The policy will be theirs ; by its wisdom, and by the method in which they administer the new law, they will be judged when they come to render an account of their stewardship to the next Parliamentary Commission. There remains of course the possibility that Ministers may not be able to get their policy accepted by the legislature or to obtain their consent to the proposals for financing it. In that event, it will be for the Governor to decide whether he should dismiss his Ministers, or the Minister for Education, as having lost the confidence of the council. By such action, however, the position of the executive council would not be affected.

Let us now examine a converse and equally

hypothetical case, in which the initiative is taken by the other half of the government. Impressed by the growth of agrarian unrest, the Governor in his executive council, after all the necessary inquiries, proposes a new system of tenant's occupancy right against the landlord, with compensation for ejectment, and so on. By a slight straining of his commission, the Minister who has Agriculture in his portfolio might argue that his department is concerned and demand a conference of the full government to discuss the scheme. This, however, would hardly be necessary; for in all matters of such moment the Governor would naturally wish to have Ministers with him, and would not stand on the strict letter of constitutional form. There would in practice be many discussions between the two halves of the government, both on the policy itself and on its major details. In the event of the Governor deciding to go on with it, the whole responsibility for arguing it in the legislature would rest on the executive council. If Ministers were converted to the policy, their support and influence in the council would be of great value; if they were not converted, there would presumably be a convention by which they would at least abstain from speaking or voting against the scheme. At this point, however, the procedure in our two hypothetical cases diverges. Should the legislature reject the tenant right scheme, the Ministers have no responsibility. If they had supported it and failed, the Governor does not regard them as having forfeited the confidence of the council, and no question arises of replacing them. But what the Governor has to decide is whether he will persevere with his land policy in the teeth of his legislature. Provided he is satisfied that the law is essential to the discharge of his responsibilities for the well-being of the peasantry, he will make the Act under his special statutory powers, and submit it through the regular channels for His Majesty's approval. As every Act made in this way must be laid before both Houses of Parliament, any member who considers that the Governor has improperly exercised his special powers has an opportunity of drawing attention to the case by the ordinary procedure of moving an address to His Majesty for the disallowance of the measure.

This brief sketch of the probable procedure in these two cases may enable you, better than quotations from reports or standing orders, to see how it is hoped to escape from the dilemma which threatened to impale dyarchy. No single compartment in administration is absolutely watertight. Very rarely indeed can a decision be taken in one without in some degree affecting the operations of another. And yet, if this argument were final, there would never be any devolution of ultimate authority by the supreme central power. It is very closely analogous to the stark problem which ever sits behind the saddle of the British Commonwealth itself. How is the independence of a Dominion to be accommodated with the supreme authority of the British Parliament? What is to happen when the interests or foreign relations of England conflict with those of any of her overseas partners? *Solvitur ambulando.* And in the same spirit of compromise we believe that the administration of an Indian province can for the present be conducted by two separate authorities, provided they are moderated and kept in touch with each other by the Governor, provided also that each honourably observes the conditions of the experiment. If unfortunately Ministers were to manipulate their transferred powers with a view to acquiring control over the reserved subjects, or if the Executive Council were to administer the reserved departments so as to curtail the transferred powers, the conditions of the experiment would not be observed and Parliament would have to interfere. Thus dyarchy, besides being a constitutional novelty, is a high test of human nature.

In giving illustrations of the working of the dual system of government, I placed before you two cases of somewhat high policy. The daily work of the government is full of minor matters of policy and routine, in which the duty of harmony and the principle of consultation are just as valid as in the weightier problems, though they take less formal shape. In order that the Governor may be kept aware of such matters, all orders and proceedings of both halves of his government come before him in weekly schedules. But there is also a traditional and very valuable usage in India, which gives the permanent heads of departments regular access to the Governor and lays on them the duty of bringing to his notice all business in their respective departments which they consider he ought to know about. This procedure, puzzling though it is to many observers, has manifest advantages in the new regime.

I have left to the last the one subject in which, above all others, the risk of discord between the two halves of the government is most to be apprehended. It is finance. How grave is the danger will be apparent when you consider the position of the provincial exchequer. It is a reservoir into which flow all the taxation imposed and revenue collected by both halves of the government, but there is no prescription of the quota which each must provide. It is also the reservoir from which both halves of the government draw for the charges of their administration ; but there is no limitation on the share which either may extract. Add to this that Ministers, in order to retain their hold over the legislature, are ever tempted to press, on the one hand for reduced taxation, on the other for higher expenditure on the more popular services under their control ; while the executive council are beset by the rising tide of charges for the less popular, but equally necessary, duties for which they are answerable. Can the possibilities of confusion and conflict go farther ?

Impressed by these fears, the Government of India, while the new Constitution was on the anvil, urged insistently the adoption of a system which became known as the "Separate Purse." This was to be an arrangement by which each half of the government would have its own treasury, or rather its own side of the treasury. Each would receive the revenue derived from its own departments, and from that revenue it would have to meet the expenses of its own departments. If it required more money, it would be responsible for promoting its own taxation measures. It would prepare a self-contained Budget for its own half of the administration, which would be amalgamated into a consolidated Budget for the province. At the outset, however, allowance would have to be made for the absence of any theoretical symmetry in such a partition. Neither the reserved nor the transferred group of departments could be expected to be so accommodating as precisely to finance itself. The executive council, by virtue of their control of certain big heads of revenue, such as land revenue, would have more money than has normally been required in the past for the services they administer; whereas Ministers saddled with heavy spending departments, such as education, would not have funds enough for their ordinary needs. Equilibrium could be procured by letting Ministers have a fixed subsidy from the reserved revenues, or a half or a third or some other fractional share of some specific item in those revenues. The adjustment to be made in this way could be ascertained in the first instance by an independent inquiry, almost on statistical averages of the respective departmental receipts and outgoings. It might be desirable to revise the adjustment periodically; but in the intervals it would be the business of each half of the government, having been started with a reasonable provision of funds, to devote its energies to developing its own sources of revenue, in order to meet the expenses of its own administrative improvements.

In defence of the Separate Purse the arguments were obvious. In the knowledge that it would enjoy the fruit of its own labours, each half of the government would have a stimulus to get the best out of its own sources of revenue. It would be able to lay out its policy in advance for a series of years, without fear that those sources could ever be plundered by the other half. Its responsibility for raising fresh taxation and the uses to which it is put would always be clearly before the electorate. The yearly struggle, or even wrangle, for funds out of a joint exchequer at Budget times would be avoided, and, generally speaking, the temptation to one side of the government to meddle with the business of the other would be minimised.

These views were vigorously combated by the then Secretary of State and the Indian witnesses who appeared before the parliamentary joint committee. What appealed to Mr. Montagu was that the training of Ministers in financial responsibility would be incomplete, and their appreciation of the administrative problems of the full government would be only partial, unless they had a voice in the settlement of the provincial Budget as a whole. To the educative effect of the Joint Purse, the Indian politician frankly added another and more powerful consideration. For him the Joint Purse was a symbol of control, as opposed to mere influence: and he contended that the time had come to give the representatives of the people a real power in the allocation of revenues and the imposition of taxes.

It is arguable that there was some confusion of ideas; but the controversy is dead now, and I need not disturb its ashes. What Parliament accepted in the end was a compromise. The portfolio of Finance is to be in the hands of a member of the executive council. The Budget will be prepared by the full government in consultation, under the Governor's guidance, without any earmarking of separate revenues. If fresh taxation is needed, it will be discussed by the full government ; and both halves will be induced, if possible, to unite in justifying it before the legislature. But if, in framing the Budget in any year, the Governor is unable to get his executive council and his Ministers to agree on the apportionment of funds between their respective spheres, he will have power, either at his own discretion or with the assistance of an independent arbiter, to "allocate the revenue and balances of the province between reserved and transferred subjects, by specifying the fractional proportions of the revenue and balances which shall be assigned to each class of subject." This allocation may run until a year after the next general election, when a fresh attempt will be made to get a Budget by agreement.

Having now tried to show you the strength and weakness of dyarchy in its everyday working, I turn from the provinces to the central government. It is a curious and interesting example of the psychology of constitution-making. Finding themselves, as I explained in my last lecture, threatened with the anomaly of leaving the central government in India the only unregenerate link in the administrative chain, the designers of the new scheme were in a somewhat serious quandary. On one side the insufficiency of the old regime beset them, as well as the claims of symmetry in the new constitutional edifice. On the other side they had taken their stand on the imperative duty of keeping the central power, the authority to which the country looks for external defence and internal order, free from any of the weaknesses that might accompany the experimental changes in the provinces. The former consideration was fatal to the *status quo*, the latter to dualism: for whatever merits dualism may have, it cannot pretend, while so near the embryo, to operate with the same promptitude and vigour as a unitary government. What, then, was left except to democratise the legislature and make the executive responsible to it? Such a step would obviously have gone far beyond anything that had been found possible in the provinces; and yet no alternative presented itself. So a compromise was effected and the first step was adopted, a democratic legislature, but not the second, a responsible executive. Back we had come to the position which we had spent so much powder and shot in destroying when the National Congress occupied it, the position into which the Morley-Minto scheme seemed forcing us, and which we had hastened to abandon as untenable. *Plus ça change plus c'est la même chose.* The central government in India, however we embroider it, is composed of an irresponsible legislature and an irremovable executive.

The Legislative Assembly or Lower House consists of 144 Members: 104 elected, 26 officials, and 14 non-officials nominated by the Viceroy. Of the elected members, 47 represent Hindus, 28 Moslems, 8 Europeans, 2 Sikhs, 6 the land-holding classes, and 2 Indian commerce; while there are 4 members for Burma, 1 for Berar, 1 for Delhi; and 5 "fancy" constituencies. The franchise is higher than for the provincial legislatures. In the province which I formerly used as an exemplar, the qualifications are an income of £66 13*s.* 4*d.*, or a house rent of £12, or the holding of land which is rented or taxed at £10 a year. The Council of State, or Upper House, is 60 strong, with 34 elected members and not more than 20 officials, the remainder being private persons nominated by the Viceroy. The constituencies are on somewhat similar racial and territorial lines to those in the Lower House; but the franchises are quite different. In the first place, the property qualifications are high; an income of £666, or the payment of half that sum in land revenue, is required in the province I have cited before, and still higher figures obtain in some of the others. In the second place, certain personal qualifications are accepted: learning, as proved by fellowship of a University or membership of its Senate; experience in public affairs, acquired in a legislature or as chairman or vice-chairman of a municipal or district board; or commercial ability, as shown by having been president of a Chamber of Commerce or of a co-operative central society. The purpose was to secure an electorate with a senatorial mind, and councillors with the qualities of the Elder Statesmen.

Here, then, we have the first measure by which the framers of the constitution hoped to differentiate their new structure from the discarded principle. The Council of State would check any attempts by the more democratic Lower House to paralyse the official executive. To this end it is armed with certain powers. It can of course reject or amend a law passed by the Assembly. If that body expostulates, the council can reason with it in conference and ultimately throw its weight into voting on the measure in a joint sitting of the two chambers. Should the council consent to a measure which the Viceroy certifies as "essential for the safety, tranquillity, or interests" of India, the Viceroy may forthwith make an Act of it even if the Assembly has rejected it. In matters financial, however, its attitude correctly follows our own Parliament Act. The Budget is laid before it, but not voted by it: and it has no power to alter any amendments made, or to restore any grants refused, by the Assembly. Thus far, the Upper House has not justified any exaggerated hopes that may have been formed of its moderating influence in a crisis. The Assembly has proved tenacious of its own privileges; and in a joint sitting the Council of State would rarely, if ever, turn the tide against a high wave of nationalist feeling. But the principle of a second chamber has been established for India; and if second chambers ever come into their own again in this iconoclastic world, they may have a future in that country as the constitution develops and matures.

Not on this somewhat debilitated weapon alone does the central executive in India depend for its defence against possible aggression by its legislature; for the Viceroy is left with certain overruling powers which I mentioned briefly in my last lecture. He may veto a Bill. He may stop the further progress of any Bill or amendment which he certifies to affect the safety or tranquillity of the country. Or, if he wishes a Bill to pass and both chambers reject it, he may make an Act of it without their help, subject to no exception being taken by Parliament when he submits it for His Majesty's assent. On the financial side, the legislature has no direct voice in the matter of supply for the army, foreign relations, the public debt, and a somewhat extended Consolidated Fund. Should supply for other purposes be refused, the Viceroy has a discretion to appropriate it; and in emergency he can authorise any expenditure which may be necessary for the safety and tranquillity of the country. In this explanation I have sometimes used the term Viceroy for short, when the authority who actually functions is the Governor-General in Council.

You have now had under review the panoply of the central executive. Does it render that body invulnerable? Experience so far suggests a negative reply: it has only demonstrated once more how ineffective is any ingenuity of the draftsman to harmonise two incompatible principles. In March last the executive framed military estimates which the legislature resented as being an unreasonably heavy burden on the taxpayer. It could not reject them however, it could not even discuss them; and up to this point they were quite safe. But the matter did not end here: for, in order to balance the Budget fresh taxation was required, and this the Assembly refused to pass. It would have been open to the Viceroy to impose the new taxes under his overruling power, for presumably he was convinced, before he proposed it, that the military expenditure was essential to the safety and tranquillity of India. He did not exercise his special power: and a compromise was effected by which the army estimates will be reduced and the taxation proposals are abated. A similar impasse need never be far off when the executive has to put forward unpopular measures; and the way out may not always be easy.

Here, then, we arrive at what I called the psychology of Constitution-making. Those who threw the central government into this particular mould were sufficiently alive to the inevitable consequences: they themselves had fully disclosed them in their criticism of the Congress-League scheme. Statutory safeguards may "have the gift of prophecy.

and understand all mysteries and all knowledge"; but they will not make things easy for an executive which looks for its mandate elsewhere than from the powerful legislature to which it is tied, nor will they cultivate the sense of responsibility in a legislature which is always liable to be overruled by its executive. "It should be understood from the beginning," reported Lord Selborne's committee on one of the overruling provisions in the Act, "that this power of the Governor-General in Council is real, and that it is meant to be used if and when necessary." Unimpeachable as a statement of theory, this provides the Viceroy with little guidance when the pinch of practice comes. He uses his arbitrary powers. The legislature counters by rejecting his next measure or refusing funds. The bludgeon has to be employed again: and the cumulative process goes on until deadlock ensues and a whirlwind of popular agitation sends everybody scurrying in search of an amended Constitution. When I was describing the arrangements in the provinces I did not deal with this aspect of the case, though it presents itself there with the same features, if with minor emphasis. The Governor's relations with his legislature in regard to reserved subjects differ in degree, but not in kind, from the Viceroy's relations with the central legislature in regard to all his business. On paper each of them has a wide discretion and an indefeasible authority. In practice each of them must walk warily indeed if he is to avoid a habit of conflict which may render the whole scheme of reform nugatory. For the Governor the position is eased by the existence of a field in which the will of the legislature is supreme, and where accordingly it can exercise its administrative ambitions. For the Viceroy's protection there is no such safety valve.

These implications were promptly realised by the Indian politician, and published on the housetops while the new constitution was still hot from the anvil. Did the draftsmen of the constitution not realise them also? I think we must assume that they certainly did, and that they had a definite purpose. That purpose was clearly to habituate the executive, even in discharging their own responsibilities, to rely more and more upon the support of their legislatures, and less and less upon the support of the British Parliament accorded through the Secretary of State. Under the old dispensation, if a Viceroy proposed to introduce a new policy, he had to persuade the Secretary of State of the necessity for it and of its wisdom ; he had also to get the Secretary of State's consent to the measures for financing it. Under the new dispensation the Secretary of State will be difficult to persuade, unless the scheme has first obtained the blessing of the Indian legislature. The Viceroy of the future will consequently tend, in increasing measure, to consult Indian opinion first, and to count on its support rather than on the academic approval of Whitehall or Westminster. In precisely similar fashion, the provincial Governors will come to lean on their local legislatures rather than on the secretariats at Delhi. Thus, under a puzzling constitutional form, there is being effected a remarkable transference of power, or at least of influence so significant as to be barely distinguishable from power. Whether Parliament appreciated the extent to which it is divesting itself of authority over India, may safely be doubted. But it is in this undemonstrative fashion that the future polity of the British Commonwealth is being established.

Before leaving the central government, I ought to explain briefly a peculiar feature in its finances which has recently attracted some attention. Under the old system, there was a complicated adjustment of revenue between the central government and the provinces. The former was unable, from the departments under its own control, to secure an income sufficient for their expenditure; and it had accordingly to eke out its resources by taking a share of what the provinces collected. With changed conditions, this arrangement became untenable. Financial autonomy was demanded by the provinces, and the idea of paying tribute to the central government was scouted. At the same time the latter could not balance its own Budget, and a committee of arbitration was appointed to solve the problem. As postulates the committee was instructed to take the rupee at two shillings and military expenditure at a fixed and very moderate maximum; both of which assumptions have been entirely upset by subsequent events. This much, however, in parenthesis. The outcome of the arbitrament was to fix a sum which each province should now contribute to the expenses of the central government, having regard to the present state of their respective finances; and also to settle the ratio to be borne in future by each province in the deficit of the central exchequer, on the understanding that the central government will take such steps for expanding its own resources as will permit of the gradual reduction and the final extinction of contributions from the provinces. The subject is a little complicated, and I mention it only because some of the provinces are already in rebellion against their contributions. The general difficulty of making ends meet, in a period of unexampled financial depression, has greatly increased the problems of the new Constitution.

Regarding the last stage in the official hierarchy, the India Office, there is little to be said. At one time, as I have mentioned earlier, extensive changes were contemplated; but for the present they have not been pursued. By law the Secretary of State, as agent for the British Parliament, remains the proper authority to "superintend, direct, and control all acts, operations, and concerns which relate to the government or revenues of India"; and the Governor-General in Council, in his control of the civil and military Government of India, "is required to pay due obedience to all such orders as he may receive from the Secretary of State" (sections 2 and 33 of the Consolidation Act). Contrast this with the position to-day in actual practice of the Secretary of State for the Colonies in relation to a self-governing Dominion. The gradual movement from the former position to the latter will be the measure of India's constitutional emancipation; and we may be sure that it will not be effected by formal legislation. That has not been the British habit. In the present case the Secretary of State has been authorised by the Act of 1919 to restrict by rule the exercise of his own powers of control; and inasmuch as the rules which he makes under this paradoxical provision have to receive the tacit assent of both Houses of Parliament, it may be taken that they represent the extent to which Parliament, without any fuss or declamation, relinquishes its own authority over the Indian administration. The rules made thus far restrict the Secretary of State, in his control of those departments which have been transferred to Ministers, to certain broad considerations, such as the safeguarding of Imperial interests or settling quarrels between two provinces. This is the first charter of independence for the popular half of the dual governments in the provinces.

But alongside of this curious, but simple, process of statutory devolution there is at work a more subtle operation, the gradual abdication of authority over the reserved departments and over those which remain with the central executive. For them the Secretary of State continues fully responsible, inasmuch as they are under official control. As I have tried to show you, however, the tendency of the new Constitution is to throw the official executives into the arms of their own legislatures. It will be for the Secretary of State to relax his intervention accordingly. To some extent he can do this by Orders in Council, delegating authority in some of the many questions which formerly had to be referred from India for his sanction. But in the main the devolution of his power will take the form of a growing reluctance to interfere in matters in which the official executive moves with the concurrence of its legislature. In this way the ingenious cycle of the indirect transference of responsibility is completed, and the way is paved for the evolution of a new type of government, such as I shall attempt to forecast next Wednesday.

After hearing my story of the new machinery and its working, you may be thinking that there is much in it that is tentative and speculative and precarious. Perhaps there is. But if I may speak in a parable, this is how I picture to myself what might have happened if we had taken no risks. I picture to myself a vast and complicated engine, with many levers and switches and gauges, some of them difficult to manipulate, others relatively easy. It is installed inside a great dome of glass. Within the dome are a small company of selected experts, industrious, devoted, who work the engine and keep all the keys of its mechanism in their own hands. Without the dome are a growing crowd of workmen, comparatively inexpert but anxious to learn. They are hungry to be allowed inside, instead of flattening their noses against the glass as they watch the wheels go round. Some of them want to study the engine, others aim at trying their prentice hands on the simpler levers. As they tell each other how it is they who paid for the engine, and it is they who live by the electricity it generates, their enthusiasm for taking some share in the working of it waxes bolder. I picture to myself what will happen if the experts within refuse them admission. I can see the angry men outside at last picking up stones and smashing the glass dome, and in the process irretrievably damaging the great engine. And I wonder if this would have been better than what we have courageously attempted.

LECTURE VI

ITS OUTLOOK

WHEN a Constitution has not been more than eighteen months in existence, it may seem as premature to attempt a forecast of its future as to estimate its results. But certain of its more obvious tendencies have been hinted at in my previous lectures, and the human interest in the experiment lies largely in our hopes for its development. Let us examine some of the more immediate problems before it, and some aspects of the raw material from which the new machinery will have to manufacture the future political life of India.

Let us first, however, dispose of one or two misunderstandings which have recently gained currency. When the recent controversy over military expenditure was in progress at Delhi between the central executive and their legislature, perfectly intelligent critics went about describing it as an example of the risks and weakness of dyarchy. Now, risks enough there are in dyarchy, as we have seen: but this peculiar sort of trouble is not one of them. There is no dyarchy in the central government of India, and the difficulties over the army estimates were the difficulties of a unified executive dealing with a legislature to which it is not fully and finally responsible. They had no connection with the provincial system of dualism. Again, in a book of the highest authority which was published a few months ago a province in India is quoted as having " skipped dyarchy " in the sense, as I gather, that its executive council and its Ministers believe themselves to be working together as a unified government. This indicates another misunderstanding. The nearer that a provincial governor can get, by the freest and frankest consultation between the two halves of his government, to an agreement on all broad lines of policy, the better for his own comfort. But that does not mean the short-circuiting or dissolution of dyarchy. For even a unified government is not an autocracy: and the moment that the Secretary of State pulls up the Governor in Council for going too far in one direction, or the legislature pulls up Ministers for going too far in the other, the mechanism of dyarchy has to be brought into action. Moreover, the law requires every order of the government to be authenticated as made by one or other half of the government ; and no plea of consultation can exempt the authority which has set its seal to a particular policy from being exclusively answerable for that policy, or from being judged by it at the next decennial Parliamentary inquiry.

Even from such misunderstandings as those to which I have referred, however, there is a lesson to be learned. It is that, during the seven or eight years before the first parliamentary committee, a good many edges will be worn off the Constitution. It will not be quite so smartly tailored as when it first left Committee Room A at Westminster. One test, though not of course the supreme test, of its daily working will be its reasonable elasticity : and this is ensured by the wide jurisdiction of the rule-making power, which may be exercised in minor matters with the tacit, and in major matters with the express, assent of Parliament. Whatever history may have to say on the broader statesmanship of the experiment, we need not apprehend that it will be crippled by any minor defect of mechanism.

One direction in which it seems likely that pressure for change will frequently be exerted is the enlargement of the bounds of the popular half of the dual government in the provinces; in other words, the removal of more departments from the control of the executive council and their addition to the list of departments under the control of Ministers. The present lines of demarcation were settled, after prolonged inquiry by a committee in India and careful investigation by a joint committee of both Houses of Parliament, and were formally approved by resolutions of both Houses. But young governments like young animals are impatient, and there already are signs of a disposition to demand that the transference of power shall proceed at a more rapid pace than the Act permits. This of course could technically be effected by amending the existing rules; and if the Secretary of State were not urged by the standing committee of Parliament on Indian affairs, or if he rejected their advice, to get a formal resolution of Parliament, it would be within his discretion merely to "lay" the new rules on the chance of their being accepted without debate. The amendment would take the simple form of cancelling certain entries in the lists of "reserved" subjects in the provinces and inserting them in the list of "transferred" subjects. It is arguable, however, whether Parliament, though it cannot bind itself, intended this procedure to be adopted, and probably it would object if such a course were attempted. What the Act provides is the appointment, about the end of 1929, of a commission to inquire "into the working of the system of government, the growth of education, and the development of representative institutions, in British India," and to report "whether and to what extent it is desirable . . . to extend, modify, or restrict the degree of responsible government then existing therein." It is natural to suppose that Parliament would prefer to move on the advice of this commission, and not otherwise. It is also legitimate to anticipate that the commission will conduct its inquiry in the spirit of the notable preamble of the Act, which declares that in the development of self-governing institutions Parliament "must be guided by the co-operation received from those on whom new opportunities of service will be conferred, and by the extent to which it is found that confidence can be reposed on their sense of responsibility." On this weighty issue the fruits of actual administration will presumably be accepted as evidence, rather than forensic assertions. A speeding-up of the process of transference at the present moment would thus be a definite reversal of the policy enacted by Parliament in 1919.

Many Englishmen, searching for guidance as to the probable lines of normal growth, apart from formal changes in the Constitution, would turn for enlightenment to the party system and the prospects of its evolution. When we plume ourselves, as we justly do, on the part which the party system plays in the oxygenation of political life in England, we are apt to forget how long it took to acquire that salutary character. We can hardly expect it to emerge forthwith in a new Constitution, and particularly in a country with the fissiparous social traditions of India. In fact there have as yet been no trustworthy indications of how it will shape. Outside the legislatures, the most prominent political issue is co-operation or non-co-operation with the British Government in working the new Constitution. Obviously this is not an issue which can enter the legislatures and become the basis for the formation of parties. Non-co-operationists must, on their own hypothesis, remain outside and provide an argument, if there is anything in the preamble of the Act, for arresting or even reversing the advance to responsible government. If on the other hand the party, as seems to be generally expected, change their tactics and put up candidates for the councils at the next general election, then *cadit quæstio*, and non-co-operation is dead in its present form.

Within the legislatures, a pseudo-party-system is suggested by the existence of communal representation. When in every chamber in the country you have so many seats reserved for Hindus who are to be elected exclusively by Hindu voters, and so many seats reserved for Moslems who are to be elected exclusively by Moslem voters, it would seem inevitable that the Hindu members and the Moslem members should form themselves into definite groups for the promotion of the interests of their respective co-religionists. Those of you who have read the report of Mr. Montagu and Lord Chelmsford will remember how hard they fought against the principle of separate representation for religions. They argued that it would be opposed to the teaching of history, that it would perpetuate class divisions, and that it would stereotype relations which in the past have been embittered by mutual suspicion and contempt. During their inquiry in India they laboured strenuously for agreement on a territorial rather than a racial principle. It was the unmistakable sincerity and force of Mohammedan feeling which defeated them. Among the common people, as we shall see later, the natural instinct to live a peaceful life is subject to violent theological rupture at regular intervals; and each side looks to the State for protection against the other. The more educated classes cherish the same apprehension in a form more subtle and more related to the balance of political power and public office, which the Moslems believe to be slipping steadily from their hands. Both sides felt that the Lucknow compact of 1916, by which the National Congress and the Moslem League agreed in an arithmetical valuation of their respective interests in a new constitution, was a measure of protection to which at all risks they must cling. They were also intensely proud of it as a supreme effort of magnanimity. A constitutional principle, however questionable in the abstract, is difficult to resist when it is backed by the insistence of the proletariate as well as by urgent political expediency. And thus separate representation for Moslems was reluctantly conceded, as it had been in 1906 by Lord Minto and again in 1909 by Lord Morley. The Sikhs followed with a plea which their battle services made equally unanswerable. The principle is established for the present.

If experience is required of sectarianism as a basis for party politics, we can provide it near home. In India it would in all probability be equally unfortunate. The first essential to the healthy give-and-take of public life is that men should forget the bitterness which for nearly one thousand years has surged between Hinduism and Islam. Clearly not a simple proposition, but one which their recent union in the demand for reform may bring nearer than any formal efforts at conciliation. For the moment at any rate there are no signs of acute sectarian grouping. It will probably be averted so long as we stand between the provinces and full responsible government. When that consummation arrives, the question will be whether the electorate has been sufficiently educated to postpone religious susceptibilities to a common patriotism.

Looking elsewhere for the germ of a party system we do not seem to find it where by some has been thought possible, in the clash between the interests of town and country. In reality there is no inherent conflict between the two. Industrialism is still in its infancy, and there can be no corresponding grievance to that which the corn duties furnished in England. Urban and rural interests indeed would at present be content to unite in a policy of general protection with moderate export duties. While, however, we get no help in this direction, I think we have recently seen two straws in the wind. To one I have already alluded. A provincial legislature has recently been divided over a question of tenant-right. The landlord interest went solid against certain concessions which were urged on behalf of the tenants by a group of members calling themselves liberals and belonging to the legal and other professions. The second portent comes from Madras, where the non-Brahman community, or, more correctly, the Hindus of the higher castes other than the Brahman caste, have agitated with some success for the rectification of what they allege is the exclusive and unduly favoured position secured by Brahmans in the public life of that province. These two incidents point to the possibility, though not necessarily immediate or even near, of a party cleavage on lines very familiar to us: privilege *versus* rights, or an authoritarian order of society *versus* a demand for social liberty.

Speculation on this subject, however, is

naturally indefinite at so early a stage. It will become more feasible if and when the present party of non-co-operation enter the councils. Should their basic principles inspire a party movement—and I am convinced that they have roots too deep in the mind of Hinduism to be content with a less vigorous growth—we might then expect the makings of a weighty and permanent party issue: orthodoxy *versus* progress. I am very conscious how wrong it would be to use these terms as necessarily antithetic; but I cannot think of any other single pair of words which would express the picture. On the one side there would be a party which would find the canons of political life and social organisation in the religious or philosophic manuals of the past. In some respects they would be puritanical, aiming at greater simplicity of life and creeds. They would probably favour elaborate legal regulation of social relations, an exclusive policy in foreign affairs and tariffs and, generally, a reversion to certain older ideals in economics and statecraft. They would base themselves on authority rather than on reason; they would lean rather to established usage than to innovation. On the other side would be a party less disposed to ceremonial orthodoxy in their faiths, and looking for more light in new scientific conceptions than in accepted dogmas. They would seek to blend the essentials of Indian life with whatever they could adapt of Western ideals. Their inclination would be towards closer relations with the rest of the British Commonwealth and an industrial policy. They would adopt theories of personal, fiscal, and social liberty. Both parties would be intensely Nationalist, but the radical divergence between them would open slowly out, as concrete cases arose to emphasise it. Meanwhile the two straws which we watched a few minutes ago seemed to be moving in the directions in which these winds of doctrine might be expected ultimately to blow.

Turning from those somewhat nebulous conjectures regarding political parties, we come to the type of government and of governmental policy which seems likely to emerge out of the new conditions. In my last lecture I tried to show you how, even in the departments still under its immediate direction, Parliament had, perhaps unwittingly, established a halfway house between the maintenance of the old British policy in India and the adoption of a definitely Nationalist policy. We saw how the British authorities in India are taught, by the position into which the new Constitution has thrust them, to turn less and less to the Secretary of State for guidance and support, and to attune themselves more and more to the wishes of their own legislatures. We observed the habit of compromise already growing, and I think we recognised that a blending of ideals is on its way to replace our former insistence on our own administrative principles. Between now and the first decennial inquiry, unless the Constitution is to be always running on to the rocks, we shall witness a steady orientalisation of the government, side by side with a steady Indianisation of the public services; and in the process our own British officials will be participants. There is no use in blinking the plain fact. That is what will happen, whatever the party system may be. For the protection of our own ideals we must look, first, to the success with which our teaching and example have already impressed them on the convictions of the intelligence of India; and then to the skill with which, during this period of transition, our officials in India foster the sense of responsibility against the spirit of extravagance. And in the end it will be for Parliament to require that the process be not unduly one-sided; that the sacrifice of principle be not made wholly by us, and that there be no sacrifice of the vital principles of good government on which our Empire rests. With those safeguards we may live to see the administration of India transformed into a real national government, long before full responsible government by the people themselves is achieved. Concrete stages in this gradual transformation may not be sufficiently definite for description ; but one or two measurable changes are reasonably certain. The first, already started, is a campaign of economy, which will gradually strip India of the scientific establishments created for the enforcement of advanced standards in educational, sanitary, veterinary policy, and the like. Another example is the almost certain abolition of periodical revisions of the land revenue, at least in the provinces where there are landlords intermediary between the cultivator and the State. To this it is possible that Parliament would not object, if it receives adequate assurances against the abuses which prevail in Bengal where the assessments are already in perpetuity. Another tendency will be the substitution, wherever possible, of indirect for direct taxation : there being no financial heresy on which the Indian mind is more irrevocably set. And finally, a protective tariff is gradually being built up, and the cotton excise for which Lancashire has so tenaciously fought will have to be abandoned. It will be understood that, in this forecast, no account is taken of the changes which Ministers will initiate in the policy of their own transferred departments—changes with which Parliament has indirectly pledged itself not to interfere. They will be specially noteworthy, it may be assumed, in the fields of education and public health.

In this hurried sketch of the immediate future I have merely given you impressions which could be gleaned by anyone who has followed the public form of Indian political leaders during the last generation. It has long been apparent in what directions they would alter our lines of policy if they came into power: and it requires no seer's vision to forecast the more imminent changes they will introduce. It was not of course by reason of conversion to the views of the Indian Nationalist that we put him in a position to enforce those views. It was in order to make him the vehicle for bringing democratic practice into India; and thus we arrive at the particular window from which the new Constitution looks out upon the most interesting phase of its new task. In the distance on which it gazes is the vision of an intelligent electorate, warmed by the democratic principles of liberty and brotherhood, and shaping its power to the ends of a common patriotism. But the paths which lead to that millennium are long and full of difficulty. In surveying them we come, as I promised at the outset, into close quarters with the human material of the new experiment.

The first, and by far the most important, stage in treating this material is to educate the electorate of the future. It is not only that education is an essential preliminary to the intelligent use of the vote, to the dilution of that oligarchy which, according to some of its critics, the new Constitution is in danger of setting up. Education is in an even more imperative sense the first of India's problems, as by education alone can India vanquish the forces which are hostile to the growth of any true democratic spirit. And the task is gigantic. We saw that only 6 per cent. of the people respond to the most elementary test of literacy; and we should probably agree that until that figure is multiplied four or five times there can be no real popular basis for the new governments. But an extension of such magnitude will mean a generation of hard work and heavy outlay. The problem of financing it alone, particularly when money is so badly needed in almost every other direction, will be one of the heaviest burdens on the new regime and one of its severest tests. Yet until this problem is faced and overcome, the Constitution will remain open to the reproach, which I have already quoted, of transferring India from an alien but experienced bureaucracy to an indigenous and inexperienced oligarchy.

Ignorance, however, is only one, though unquestionably the key to most, of the obstacles which we saw on the path to India's future. The anti-democratic forces in life are probably more abundant in India than in any other great country that has ever launched an attack upon them. They have a deeper hold upon the people, a hold so firm that none of us will live to see their expulsion. Merely to deflect or modify them will tax the fullest strength of the new political machine, and may convert India's future standard of civilisation into a form wholly unfamiliar to us to-day.

Most urgent of all national duties, though not necessarily most difficult, is the diversion into healthier channels of the energy which India now dissipates in the *odium theologicum*. In our own experience a life of vigorous sectarian polemic is not inconsistent with patriotic purpose; and the same is true of India in regard to its minor religious schisms. But the differences between Moslem and Hindu are always capable of shattering the public peace. For nine days out of every ten there is no reason why the two communities should not live amicably side by side, and they do. They work together, play together, trade with each other, do almost anything together except intermarry. But there are two battle-cries at the sound of which all goodwill ceases and the common people rally under their separate religious standards. One is idolatry, the other is the cow. No Mussulman can conceal his contempt for idol-worship, or his resentment when it disturbs his own observances. When the stentorian celebrations of Hindu festivals or weddings break in, as they frequently do, upon the fervid silence of the mosque or the ceremonial mourning of certain seasons, bitterness and even violence are never far off. Again, if there is one doctrine in the Hindu faith which knows no compromise, it is the sanctity of the cow. It comes down from earliest ages, when the cow was the closest friend of our common forefathers, the progenitors, though I suppose we must no longer call them the

Aryan progenitors, of Hinduism; and it is intertwined with the heartstrings of the Hindu peasantry to-day. By a perversity which is not wholly accidental, the Moslems of Northern India have fixed on the cow as the one animal which it is fitting to slaughter, and to slaughter in considerable numbers, on a particular occasion in each year. The occasion celebrates the interrupted sacrifice of Isaac by his father Abraham on Mount Moriah: and in other Islamic countries camels, sheep, or goats are slain in the commemoration. In India the cow has become the favourite victim, partly for economic reasons with which I need not detain you, but partly also, I am afraid, because of the distress which it causes to the Hindus. It is impossible for us to assess the depth of the cumulative animosity generated from these two causes. It flares out, every now and then, in savage sporadic violence, which leaves trails of bitterness behind. It is true that the more enlightened men on both sides deplore the situation, but they cannot avoid being dragged in when trouble comes. At present their chief endeavour is to prevent outbursts of fanaticism from breaking the ranks of reform, and the restoration of order is left to the British administrator. But the more that responsibility devolves on the people themselves, the more urgent will it become to find a remedy for this evil in Indian life. When a remedy is discovered, and not till then, will it be possible to dispense with communal representation and its attendant ills.

To the Englishman, familiar with at least the theory of democracy, the chief difficulty in its application would seem to be a variety of social obstacles against which Indian reformers have long tilted in vain. He would enumerate, for example, the disadvantages of the caste system from the point of view of those equal opportunities for all men which are of the essence of democracy; he would dwell on the impediments which it offers to industrial freedom and individual enterprise. He would touch on the position of women, the general apathy that exists about their education and the remoteness, not so much of any real female franchise, about which there is no hurry, as of the exercise by women of a healthy influence on public life and morality. He would refer to economic drawbacks, mentioning some of the laws of inheritance, the infinite subdivision of property, certain pauperising tendencies of the Hindu joint family system, the abuse of religious mendicancy, the wasteful marriage customs, and so on. In his enumeration he would probably forget that it is not impossible to find analogies to several of these troubles either in our own country or in other European States which have adopted democracy as their political creed.

Be that as it may, however, his list of problems is sufficiently serious. It indicates the vastness of the task with which Indian statesmen will have to grapple under the new Constitution before they can claim that their government rests on a popular basis or that they are bringing their country into line with the older democracies of the world. Nevertheless, when they fulfil their task, I think posterity will find that India has evolved a type of national life very different from what she now possesses, but also very different from anything that we have been pressing upon her. And it will find that type of life reflected in a Constitution unlike that of any self-governing nation to-day, and bearing little resemblance to the infant which was cradled in the Act of 1919.

What sort of confederacy will the varied peoples of India then present to the world? The Montagu-Chelmsford report hazarded an answer to that question. " Our conception," it says, "of the eventual future of India is a sisterhood of States, self-governing in all matters of purely local or provincial interest. . . . Over this congeries of States would preside a central government, increasingly representative of and responsible to the people of all of them; dealing with matters, both internal and external, of common interest to the whole of India; . . . and representing the interests of all India on equal terms with the self-governing units of the British Empire. In this picture there is a place also for the Native States. It is possible that they too will wish to be associated for certain purposes with the organisation of British India." The forecast is studiously cautious, and in some respects it is already possible to touch up the picture. It seems unlikely, in the first place, that the present map of India will last until the maturity of responsible government. Somewhat haphazard in their origin, our present provinces may prove inconveniently large for management by cohesive popular governments. Local interests with a separatist tendency exist, and will come into action when the centripetal influences of official rule are relaxed. The pressure of language will operate similarly; for the use of the vernacular in debates of the legislatures and in administrative business is bound to extend, and compact linguistic areas will naturally desire to have their own administrative centres. The number of constituent States in the future British India will thus, in all probability, be considerably larger than that of the present provincial units.

In the second place, the Native States cannot but be seriously affected. Ideas have a habit of overleaping territorial boundaries, and the intellectual movement in British India will assuredly have its reactions in the adjoining States. Individual chiefs who made no disguise of their sympathy with it in its earlier stages are growing considerably exercised over its unexpected success: and the moral which some of our critics are drawing from the States will be strikingly falsified. It has recently been fashionable to cite them as evidence of the popularity in India of the strong one-man rule: and they are supposed to contrast, in its general fitness for survival, the picturesque indigenous administration with our own drab and alien government. Whatever truth there may be in the antithesis, it affords no guide to another comparison—the comparison, to wit, between an indigenous autocracy and an indigenous democracy, especially in cases where the former happens to fall short of that paternal ideal which is very definitely formulated in the Indian mind There is thus a talk of impending constitutions even in the States: and where one or two of the more adventurous lead the way, others will in time follow. For in the Chamber of Princes we have not the least momentous or pregnant of the major changes which have been recently effected. Created for the discussion of matters of common interest to the different States, it will not be able to exclude from its purview the one topic of supreme interest to them all—the growth of free institutions across their borders. The spread of the movement into the States will be watched, views exchanged, competitive schemes of concession designed. As the process develops, we may expect that the old arbitrary sway of many of the princes will be tempered by popular assemblies with increasing ambitions and powers. Free from the dynastic tradition of formal alliance with Britain, these rejuvenated communities will come to find the need for closer political relations with the administrations in British India.

It is a unique type of federation that we see in the picture as thus enlarged. It may contain some of our present provinces, while others will probably be broken up and re-grouped on an ethnical or linguistic basis. Alongside of them will be States, conterminous with or forming groups of the present Indian States. In some of them absolutism may linger ; in others the form of government may approximate to a limited monarchy ; many will probably have reached responsible government. Some new form of federal union will bind the congeries together ; some new pattern of central power will combine them in face of the outer world. The tendency of the individual States will be at first towards partition into smaller communities. Economic causes will operate later to amalgamate those into larger units ; and the responsibilities of external defence will then have to be shouldered, as well as the problems of India's relations with other Asiatic powers. Meanwhile, during the long years that will be necessary to bring this new and many-hued Dominion to maturity, who will ensure that it is kept free from external aggression and from internecine struggles, free to work out, in peace and at leisure, its novel fortunes ? Who else but the naval and military forces of the British Commonwealth ? And thus, if for no other reason, will continue our association with the greatest constitutional experiment in modern history.

The story of that experiment is now before you. Sir Courtenay Ilbert described the legal framework into which the structure of India's Constitution has to be fitted. I have tried to show you what the structure will be like and in which directions it seems disposed to expand. Sir Courtenay expressed hope and confidence in the future. That hope I respectfully echo. The Constitution which India has just received is full of novelties, and full of difficulties for all who are associated in its working. But it provides India, as no other country has been provided in history, with the choice of its own future, and our reward will be gauged by the wisdom of her choice.

APPENDICES

APPENDIX I

Preamble of the Government of India Act, 1919.

APPENDIX II

(*a*) *List of " Central " Subjects.*
(*b*) *List of Provincial " Reserved " Subjects*
(*c*) *List of Provincial " Transferred " Subjects.*

APPENDIX III

Instrument of Instructions to the Governor of a Province to which the Act applies.

APPENDIX I

PREAMBLE OF THE GOVERNMENT OF INDIA ACT, 1919

THE following is the preamble of the Government of India Act, 1919 [9 and 10 Geo. V, Ch. 101].

. . . . . .

Whereas it is the declared policy of Parliament to provide for the increasing association of Indians in every branch of Indian administration, and for the gradual development of self-governing institutions, with a view to the progressive realisation of responsible government in British India as an integral part of the empire :

And whereas progress in giving effect to this policy can only be achieved by successive stages, and it is expedient that substantial steps in this direction should now be taken :

And whereas the time and manner of each advance can be determined only by Parliament, upon whom responsibility lies for the welfare and advancement of the Indian peoples :

And whereas the action of Parliament in such matters must be guided by the co-operation received from those on whom new opportunities of service will be conferred, and by the extent to which it is found that confidence can be reposed in their sense of responsibility :

And whereas concurrently with the gradual development of self-governing institutions in the Provinces of India it is expedient to give to those Provinces in provincial matters the largest measure of independence of the Government of India, which is compatible with the due discharge by the latter of its own responsibilities :

Be it therefore enacted by the King's most Excellent Majesty, by and with the advice and consent of the Lords Spiritual and Temporal, and Commons, in this present Parliament assembled, and by the authority of the same, as follows.

. . . . . .

Here follows the Act, which exigencies of space do not allow to be printed *in extenso*. Copies can be obtained from Eyre & Spottiswoode, Ltd., through any bookseller, at a low price.

APPENDIX II

(A) LIST OF "CENTRAL" SUBJECTS

1. (*a*) Defence of India, and all matters connected with His Majesty's Naval, Military and Air Forces in India, or with His Majesty's Indian Marine Service or with any other force raised in India, other than military and armed police wholly maintained by local Governments.

(*b*) Naval and military works and cantonments.

2. External relations, including naturalisation and aliens, and pilgrimages beyond India.

3. Relations with States in India.

4. Political charges.

5. Communications to the extent described under the following heads, namely :—

(*a*) railways and extra-municipal tramways, in so far as they are not classified as provincial subjects under entry 6 (*d*) of Part C of this Appendix ;

(*b*) aircraft and all matters connected therewith ;

(*c*) inland waterways, to an extent to be declared by rule made by the Governor-General in Council or by or under legislation by the Indian legislature.

6. Shipping and Navigation, including shipping and navigation on inland waterways in so far as declared to be a central subject in accordance with entry 5 (*c*).

7. Light-houses (including their approaches), beacons, light-ships, and buoys.

8. Port quarantine, and marine hospitals.

9. Ports declared to be major ports by rule made by the Governor-General in Council or by or under legislation by the Indian legislature.

10. Posts, telegraphs and telephones, including wireless installations.

11. Customs, cotton excise duties, income-tax, salt, and other sources of all-India revenues.

12. Currency and coinage.

13. Public debt of India.

14. Savings Banks.

15. The Indian Audit Department and excluded Audit Departments, as defined in rules framed under section 96D (1) of the Act.

16. Civil law, including laws regarding status, property, civil rights and liabilities and civil procedure.

17. Commerce, including banking and insurance.

18. Trading companies and other associations.

19. Control of production, supply and distribution of any articles in respect of which control by a central authority is declared by rule made by the Governor-General in Council or by or under legislation by the Indian legislature to be essential in the public interest.

20. Development of industries, in cases where

such development by a central authority is declared by order of the Governor-General in Council, made after consultation with the local government or local governments concerned, expedient in the public interest.

21. Control of cultivation and manufacture of opium, and sale of opium for export.

22. Stores and stationery, both imported and indigenous, required for Imperial Departments.

23. Control of petroleum and explosives.

24. Geological survey.

25. Control of mineral development in so far as such control is reserved to the Governor-General in Council under rules made or sanctioned by the Secretary of State, and regulation of mines.

26. Botanical survey.

27. Inventions and designs.

28. Copyright.

29. Emigration from, and immigration into, British India, and inter-provincial migration.

30. Criminal Law, including criminal procedure.

31. Central police organisation.

32. Control of arms and ammunition.

33. Central agencies and institutions for research (including observatories) and for professional or technical training or promotion of special studies.

34. Ecclesiastical administration, including European cemeteries.

35. Survey of India.

36. Archæology.

37. Zoological Survey.

38. Meteorology.

39. Census and Statistics.

40. All-India Services.

41. Legislation in regard to any provincial subject, in so far as such subject is in Parts B and C of this Appendix stated to be subject to legislation by the Indian legislature, and any powers relating to such subject reserved by legislation to the Governor-General in Council.

42. Territorial changes, other than intra-provincial, and declaration of laws in connection therewith.

43. Regulation of ceremonial, titles, orders, precedence and civil uniform.

44. Immovable property acquired by, and maintained at the cost of, the Governor-General in Council.

45. The Public Service Commission.

46. All matters expressly excepted by the provisions of Parts B and C of this Appendix from inclusion among provincial subjects.

47. All other matters not included among provincial subjects under Parts B and C of this Appendix.

(B) LIST OF PROVINCIAL " RESERVED " SUBJECTS

1. European and Anglo-Indian Education.

2. The construction and maintenance of residences of Governors of Provinces.

3. Water supplies, irrigation and canals, drainage and embankments, water storage and water power ; subject to legislation by the Indian legislature with

regard to matters of inter-provincial concern or affecting the relations of a province with any other territory.

4. Land Revenue administration, as described under the following heads, namely :—

(*a*) assessment and collection of land revenue ;

(*b*) maintenance of land records, survey for revenue purposes, records of rights ;

(*c*) laws regarding land tenures, relations of landlords and tenants, collection of rents ;

(*d*) Courts of Wards, incumbered and attached estates ;

(*e*) land improvement and agricultural loans ;

(*f*) colonisation and disposal of Crown lands and alienation of land revenue ; and

(*g*) management of Government estates.

5. Famine Relief.

6. Forests, including preservation of game therein : subject to legislation by the Indian legislature as regards disforestation of reserved forests.

7. Land Acquisition : subject to legislation by the Indian legislature.

8. Administration of justice, including constitution, powers, maintenance and organisation of Courts of civil and criminal jurisdiction within the province ; subject to legislation by the Indian legislature as regards High Courts, Chief Courts, and Courts of Judicial Commissioners, and any Courts of criminal jurisdiction.

9. Provincial law reports.

10. Administrators General and Official Trustees ; subject to legislation by the Indian legislature.

11. Non-judicial stamps, subject to legislation by the Indian legislature, and judicial stamps, subject to legislation by the Indian legislature as regards amount of court fees levied in relation to suits and proceedings in the High Courts under their original jurisdiction.

12. Development of mineral resources which are Government property, subject to rules made or sanctioned by the Secretary of State, but not including the regulation of mines.

13. Industrial matters included under the following heads, namely :—

(*a*) factories ;
(*b*) settlement of labour disputes ;
(*c*) electricity ;
(*d*) boilers ;
(*e*) gas ;
(*f*) smoke nuisances ; and
(*g*) welfare of labour, including provident funds, industrial insurance (general, health, and accident) and housing ;

subject as to heads (*a*), (*b*), (*c*), (*d*) and (*g*) to legislation by the Indian legislature.

14. Stores and stationery required for transferred departments, subject, in the case of imported stores and stationery, to such rules as may be prescribed by the Secretary of State in Council.

15. Ports, except such ports as may be declared by rule made by the Governor-General in Council or by or under Indian legislation to be major ports.

16. Inland waterways, including shipping and navigation thereon so far as not declared by the

Governor-General in Council to be central subjects, but subject as regards inland steam-vessels to legislation by the Indian legislature.

17. Police, including railway police; subject in the case of railway police to such conditions as regards limits of jurisdiction and railway contributions to cost of maintenance as the Governor-General in Council may determine.

18. The following miscellaneous matters, namely:

(*a*) regulation of betting and gambling;

(*b*) prevention of cruelty to animals;

(*c*) protection of wild birds and animals;

(*d*) control of poisons, subject to legislation by the Indian legislature;

(*e*) control of motor vehicles, subject to legislation by the Indian legislature as regards licences valid throughout British India; and

(*f*) control of dramatic performances, and cinematographs, subject to legislation by the Indian legislature in regard to sanction of films for exhibition.

19. Control of newspapers, books and printing presses; subject to legislation by the Indian legislature.

20. Coroners.

21. Excluded areas.

22. Criminal tribes; subject to legislation by the Indian legislature.

23. European vagrancy; subject to legislation by the Indian legislature.

24. Prisons, prisoners (except State prisoners) and

reformatories; subject to legislation by the Indian legislature.

25. Pounds and prevention of cattle trespass.

26. Treasure trove.

27. Provincial Government Presses.

28. Elections for Indian and provincial legislatures subject to rules framed under sections 64 (1) and 72A (4) of the Act.

29. Regulation of medical and other professional qualifications and standards; subject to legislation by the Indian legislature.

30. Local Fund Audit, that is to say, the audit by Government agency of income and expenditure controlled by local bodies.

31. Control, as defined by rule, of members of all-India and provincial services serving within the province, and control, subject to legislation by the Indian legislature, of public services within the province, other than all-India services.

32. Sources of provincial revenue, not included under previous heads, whether—

(*a*) taxes included in the Schedules to the Scheduled Taxes Rules, or

(*b*) taxes, not included in those Schedules, which are imposed by or under provincial legislation which has received the previous sanction of the Governor-General.

33. Borrowing of money on the sole credit of the province, subject to the provisions of the Local Government (Borrowing) Rules.

34. Imposition by legislation of punishment by fine, penalty or imprisonment, for enforcing any

law of the province relating to any provincial subject; subject to legislation by the Indian legislature in the case of any subject in respect of which such a limitation is imposed under these rules.

35. Any matter which, though falling within a central subject, is declared by the Governor-General in Council to be of a merely local or private nature within the province.

36. Matters pertaining to a central subject in respect of which powers have been conferred by or under any law upon a local Government.

NOTES.—Subject No. 6 (Forests) is transferred in Bombay only.

Certain other subjects [see App. II (C)] are reserved in Assam only.

(C) LIST OF PROVINCIAL "TRANSFERRED" SUBJECTS

Subject.	Transferred in
1. Local self-government—that is to say, matters relating to the constitution and powers of municipal corporations, improvement trusts, district boards, mining boards of health and other local authorities established in the province for purposes of local self-government, exclusive of matters arising under the Cantonments Act, 1910; subject to legislation by the Indian legislature as regards (*a*) the powers of such authorities to borrow or otherwise than from a provincial Government, and (*b*) the levying by such authorities of taxation not included in Schedule II to the Scheduled Taxes Rules.	All Governors' provinces.

Subject.	Transferred in
2. Medical administration, including hospitals, dispensaries and asylums, and provision for medical education.	All Governors' provinces.
3. Public health and sanitation and vital statistics; subject to legislation by the Indian legislature in respect to infectious and contagious diseases to such extent as may be declared by any Act of the Indian legislature.	Ditto.
4. Pilgrimages within British India	Ditto.
5. Education, other than European and Anglo-Indian education, provided that— (*a*) the following subjects shall be excluded namely:— (i) the Benares Hindu University, the Aligarh Muslim University and such other Universities, constituted after the commencement of these rules, as may be declared by the Governor-General in Council to be central subjects, and (ii) Chiefs' Colleges and any institution maintained by the Governor-General in Council for the benefit of members of His Majesty's Forces or of other public servants or of the children of such members or servants; and (*b*) the following subjects shall be subject to legislation by the Indian legislature, namely:— (i) the control of the establishment, and the regulation of the constitutions and functions, of Universities constituted after the commencement of these rules, and (ii) the definition of the jurisdiction of any University outside the province in which it is situated, and (iii) for a period of five years from the date of the commencement of these rules, the Calcutta University and the control and organi-	Ditto.

Subject.	Transferred in
sation of secondary education in the presidency of Bengal.	
6. Public Works included under the following heads, namely :— (*a*) construction and maintenance of provincial buildings, other than residences of Governors of provinces, used or intended for any purpose in connection with the administration of the province on behalf of the departments of Government concerned, save in so far as the Governor may assign such work to the departments using or requiring such buildings; and care of historical monuments, with the exception of ancient monuments as defined in section 2 (1) of the Ancient Monuments Preservation Act, 1904, which are for the time being declared to be protected monuments under section 3 (1) of that Act: provided that the Governor-General in Council may, by notification in the Gazette of India, remove any such monument from the operation of this exception; (*b*) roads, bridges, ferries, tunnels, ropeways and causeways, and other means of communication, subject to such conditions as regards control over construction and maintenance of means of communication declared by the Governor-General in Council to be of military importance, and as regards incidence of special expenditure connected therewith, as the Governor-General in Council may prescribe; (*c*) tramways within municipal areas; and (*d*) light and feeder railways and extra-municipal tramways in so far as provision for their construction and management is made by provincial legislation, subject to legislation by the Indian legislature in the case of	All Governors' provinces, except Assam.

Subject.	Transferred in
any such railway or tramway which is in physical connection with a main line or is built on the same gauge as an adjacent main line.	
7. Agriculture, including research institutes, experimental and demonstration farms, introduction of improved methods, provision for agricultural education, protection against destructive insects and pests and prevention of plant diseases ; subject to legislation by the Indian legislature in respect to destructive insects and pests and plant diseases to such extent as may be declared by any Act of the Indian legislature.	All Governors' provinces.
8. Civil Veterinary Department, including provision for veterinary training, improvement of stock, and prevention of animal diseases ; subject to legislation by the Indian legislature in respect to animal diseases to such extent as may be declared by any Act of the Indian legislature.	Ditto.
9. Fisheries	All Governors' provinces, except Assam.
10. Co-operative Societies	All Governors' provinces.
11. Forests, including preservation of game therein ; subject to legislation by the Indian legislature as regards disforestation of reserved forests.	Bombay.
12. Excise, that is to say, the control of production, manufacture, possession, transport, purchase, and sale of alcoholic liquor and intoxicating drugs, and the levying of excise duties and licence fees on or in relation to such articles, but excluding, in the case of opium, control of cultivation, manufacture and sale for export.	All Governors' provinces, except Assam.
13. Registration of deeds and documents ; subject to legislation by the Indian legislature.	All Governors' provinces.
14. Registration of births, deaths and marriages ; subject to legislation by the Indian legislature for such classes as the Indian legislature may determine.	Ditto.

Subject.	Transferred in
15. Religious and charitable endowments ..	All Governors' provinces.
16. Development of industries, including industrial research and technical education.	Ditto.
17. Stores and stationery required for transferred Departments, subject, in the case of imported stores and stationery, to such rules as may be prescribed by the Secretary of State in Council.	Ditto.
18. Adulteration of food-stuffs and other articles; subject to legislation by the Indian legislature as regards import and export trade.	Ditto.
19. Weights and measures; subject to legislation by the Indian legislature as regards standards.	Ditto.
20. Libraries (other than the Imperial Library), Museums (except the Indian Museum, Imperial War Museum, and the Victoria Memorial, Calcutta) and Zoological Gardens.	Ditto.

APPENDIX III

INSTRUMENT OF INSTRUCTIONS FROM THE CROWN TO THE GOVERNORS OF PROVINCES TO WHICH THE ACT APPLIES

Whereas by the Government of India Act, provision has been made for the gradual development of self-governing institutions in British India with a view to the progressive realisation of responsible government in that country as an integral part of Our Empire ;

And whereas it is Our will and pleasure that, in the execution of the Office of Governor in and over the Presidency of Fort William in Bengal, you shall further the purposes of the said Act, to the end that the institutions and methods of government therein provided shall be laid upon the best and surest foundations, that the people of the said presidency shall acquire such habits of political action and respect such conventions as will best and soonest fit them for self-government, and that Our authority and the authority of Our Governor-General in Council shall be duly maintained ;

Now, therefore, We do hereby direct and enjoin you and declare Our will and pleasure to be as follows :—

I. You shall do all that lies in your power to maintain standards of good administration ; to encourage religious toleration, co-operation and goodwill among all classes and creeds ; to ensure the probity of public finance and the solvency of the presidency ; and to promote all measures making for the moral, social, and industrial welfare of the people, and tending to fit all classes of the population without distinction to take their due share in the public life and government of the country.

II. You shall bear in mind that it is necessary and expedient that those now and hereafter to be enfranchised shall appreciate the duties, responsibilities and advantages which spring from the privilege of enfranchisement ; that is to say, that those who exercise the power henceforward entrusted to them of returning representatives to the legislative council, being enabled to perceive the effects of their choice of a representative, and that those who are returned to the council, being enabled to perceive the effects of their votes given therein, shall come to look for the redress of their grievances and the improvement of their condition to the working of representative institutions.

III. Inasmuch as certain matters have been reserved for the administration according to law of the Governor in Council, in respect of which the authority of Our Governor-General in Council shall remain unimpaired, while certain other matters have been transferred to the administration of the Governor acting with a Minister, it will be for you so to regulate the business of the government of the presidency that, so far as may be possible, the responsibility of each for these respective classes of matters may be kept clear and distinct.

IV. Nevertheless, you shall encourage the habit of joint deliberation between yourself, your Councillors and your Ministers, in order that the experience of your official advisers may be at the disposal of your Ministers, and that the knowledge of your Ministers as to the wishes of the people may be at the disposal of your Councillors.

V. You shall assist Ministers by all the means in your power in the administration of the transferred subjects, and advise them in regard to their relations with the legislative council.

VI. In considering a Minister's advice and deciding whether or not there is sufficient cause in any case to dissent from his opinion, you shall have due regard to his relations with the legislative council and to the wishes of the people of the presidency as expressed by their representatives therein.

VII. But in addition to the general responsibilities with which you are, whether by statute or under this Instrument, charged, We do further hereby specially require and charge you :—

(1) to see that whatsoever measures are, in your opinion, necessary for maintaining safety and tranquillity in all parts of your presidency and for preventing occasions of religious or racial conflict, are duly taken, and that all orders issued by

Our Secretary of State or by Our Governor General in Council on Our behalf to whatever matters relating are duly complied with ;

(2) to take care that due provision shall be made for the advancement and social welfare of those classes amongst the people committed to your charge, who, whether on account of the smallness of their number or their lack of educational or material advantages or from any other cause, specially rely upon Our protection, and cannot as yet fully rely for their welfare upon joint political action, and that such classes shall not suffer, or have cause to fear, neglect or oppression ;

(3) to see that no order of your Government and no Act of your legislative council shall be so framed that any of the diverse interests of or arising from race, religion, education, social condition, wealth or any other circumstance, may receive unfair advantage, or may unfairly be deprived of privileges or advantages which they have heretofore enjoyed, or be excluded from the enjoyment of benefits which may hereafter be conferred on the people at large ;

(4) to safeguard all members of Our services employed in the said presidency in the legitimate exercise of their functions, and in the enjoyment of all recognised rights

and privileges, and to see that your Government order all things justly and reasonably in their regard, and that due obedience is paid to all just and reasonable orders and diligence shown in their execution ;

(5) to take care that, while the people inhabiting the said presidency shall enjoy all facilities for the development of commercial and industrial undertakings, no monopoly or special privilege which is against the common interest shall be established, and no unfair discrimination shall be made in matters affecting commercial or industrial interests.

VIII. And We do hereby charge you to communicate these Our Instructions to the Members of your Executive Council and your Ministers and to publish the same in your presidency in such manner as you may think fit.

INDEX